GUTHLAC OF CROYLAND

A Study of Heroic Hagiography

Alexandra Hennessey Olsen

UNIVERSITY
PRESS OF
AMERICA

PR
1722
.O4
1981

Copyright © 1981 by
University Press of America,Inc."
P.O. Box 19101, Washington, D.C. 20036

All rights reserved

Printed in the United States of America

ISBN: 0-8191-1981-4 (Perfect)
0-8191-1980-6 (Case)

Library of Congress Number: 81-40062

To Gary L. Olsen

Acknowledgments

I should like to express my gratitude to Professor Alain Renoir of the University of California at Berkeley and to Professors Donald C. Baker and J. D. A. Ogilvy of the University of Colorado at Boulder for reading the manuscript of this book and making helpful suggestions about it. For the views expressed in the following pages, however, I take sole responsibility. I should also like to thank Everett Wayne Whitmarsh for his careful preparation of the manuscript.

I should like to thank Oxford University Press for permission to quote from <u>The Guthlac Poems of the Exeter Book</u> and Dr. James David Mason for permission to quote from "Monsters with Human Voices: The Anthropomorphic Adversary of the Hero in Old English and Old Norse Literature."

Publication of this book was made possible by a Faculty Research Grant from the University of Denver.

Table of Contents

Chapter One
  Old English Hagiographic Poetry:
  "Fit Audience Find, Though Few"   1
    Notes to Chapter One   9

Chapter Two
  The Return of the Hero-Saint:
  A Reconsideration of Guthlac A   15
    Section A
      Homily and Hagiography:
      The Learned Background   15
    Section B
      Formula and Theme:
      The Heroic Background   25
    Section C
      The Eternal Return:
      The Mythic Background   47
    Section D
      Guthlac A: The Composite View   53
    Notes to Chapter Two   57

Chapter Three
  Guthlac B and the Cycle of History   69
    Section A
      The Orosian View of Christian
      History   69
    Section B
      Saintly Death and Heroic
      Journey   94
    Section C
      Guthlac B: The Composite View   101
    Notes to Chapter Three   105

Chapter Four
  Guthlac: A Proposed Reading of the
  Composite Poem   111

    Section A
        Epic and Hagiography:
        Medieval Unity   111
    Section B
        The Re-Sung Song   123
    Section C
        Guthlac: The Composite View   132
    Notes to Chapter Four   133

Conclusion
    The Artistry of the Guthlac Poems 141

Bibliography   143

Index   157

Chapter One
Old English Hagiographic Poetry:
"Fit Audience Find, Though Few"

    For many years, the small corpus of extant Old English poetry has been the focus of scholarly controversy centering on the means whereby the poems were composed. Many critics, following the lead of Milman Parry, Albert B. Lord, and Francis P. Magoun, Jr.,[1] believe that the poems were composed orally, whereas their opponents maintain that "there is no hard evidence to suggest"[2] that they were. The disagreement between the two schools of criticism will undoubtedly continue for many years. Nevertheless, as Donald K. Fry has pointed out, ever since "Larry Benson exploded the necessary identification of formularity and orality . . . a consensus seems to be emerging that written Old English poetry used oral forms, but no reliable test can differentiate written from oral poems."[3] In view of this emerging consensus, the time seems appropriate to re-examine those formulaic poems whose similarity to Latin models makes their oral composition seem unlikely, especially the hagiographic poems. The latter are the product of what Edward B. Irving has called "the collision of two cultures,"[4] that of formulaic Germanic verse and that of Graeco-Latin hagiography, and they have, to use Irving's terminology, a "mixed" (p. 153) nature.

    The present study discusses two poems, known to modern critics as <u>Guthlac</u> <u>A</u> and <u>Guthlac</u> <u>B</u>, which were copied consecutively in the <u>Exeter Book</u> and were presumably intended to be read as a unit. Although most critics wish to dismiss what Daniel G. Calder has described as "that medieval perspective which can see <u>Guthlac</u> <u>A</u> and <u>B</u> as one 'composite' poem,"[5] I should like to suggest that in order to do justice to the <u>Guthlac</u> poems, we must read <u>Guthlac</u> as a composite as well as reading the sections of which it is composed. <u>Guthlac</u> <u>A</u> and <u>B</u>

have themselves been read in ways which fail to do complete justice to them because modern critics have considered only part of their central technical devices. The present study considers the ways in which modern critical approaches have produced inappropriate readings of the poems and suggests that the most rewarding approach involves the use of a composite technique which considers the poems in the light both of the literary and theological legacy of the Patristic period and of the heroic Germanic vocabulary, formulas, and themes used in them. Only those who read the poems with a sympathetic understanding of both traditions are likely to assess their literary merit with some degree of objectivity.

One school of criticism has concentrated on discussing the Patristic background of the Guthlac poems, especially their legacy from hagiography. Hagiography can be approached from two different points of view: from that exemplified by the Bollandists, who are interested in authenticating works for devotional use by modern Catholics,[6] or from that exemplified by scholars like Charles W. Jones and Robert W. Hanning, who are interested in the literary merits of particular works rather than in the historicity or the religious orthodoxy thereof.[7] In a recent article,[8] I have surveyed the genre and concluded that some critics find it of little interest because they approach it with erroneous preconceptions. As a result, they criticize it for not doing what they expect it to do and fail to understand what it does. Because of their preconceptions, many Anglo-Saxonists have adopted the judgments made by the Bollandists as if the judgments were authoritative pronouncements on the literary merits of hagiography; their studies have therefore been of less value than they might otherwise have been. Some of the criticism is nevertheless extremely valuable because it demonstrates the relationship of the Old English poems to their Latin source, the Vita Sancti Guthlaci, and because it identifies intellectual and theological influences on them which would otherwise be inaccessible to a modern audience. Another school of criticism has considered only the heroic poetic devices in the poems and has generally concluded that the poems are of relatively little interest because they are not heroic in the strict sense of the word. However, such criticism has also demonstrated the technical proficiency with which the <u>Guthlac</u> poets have used the formulaic devices of composition.

In contradistinction, the composite technique approaches the poems with full realization that they make no pretense to be heroic in the strict sense of the word and that they use the heroic vocabulary to describe a different but analogous subject matter. At the same time, it approaches them with an adequate understanding of and sympathy for hagiography as a complex literary genre whose excellence cannot be easily measured, and it enables the modern reader to understand how traditional narratives have been re-cast to fit in with the aesthetic standards of a particular time, place, and language. Only one who reads Old English hagiographic poetry as a composite is able to realize that in it two different heroic traditions merge.

Throughout Christendom, including Anglo-Saxon England, hagiographic narratives kept alive not merely what Michael D. Cherniss calls "vestiges of heroic tradition"[9] but the heroic tradition itself because the saints took the places of secular heroes. In the Introduction to <u>Anglo-Saxon Saints and Heroes</u>, Clinton Albertson traces the way in which the secular Heroic Age of Anglo-Saxon England gave way to the Heroic Age of Anglo-Saxon monasticism, and he argues that Christian saints are like epic heroes: "The hagiographers are writing about heroes and in a heroic literary tradition. Achilles and Beowulf do impossible things by ordinary human standards. Heroes are larger than life, they represent an eternal essence of virtue which mediocre everyman imitates them for, and prays to receive in some measure from them. The

Greek hero was seen that way, and also the
Christian hero-saint. Behind the hero is always
a god."[10] Albertson is talking about Anglo-Latin
hagiographies, but his comments are even more
applicable to the Old English hagiographic poems,
for, as Rosemary Woolf has pointed out, "the verse
lives . . . were obviously primarily intended as
edifying substitutes for heroic poetry. . . . They
could be best appreciated by those familiar with
Old English heroic literature."[11]

    The studies of Magoun and his followers have
taught us a great deal about the composition of
heroic Germanic alliterative poetry, and there is
now almost general agreement that Old English
poetry was composed by the manipulation of formulaic half-lines.[12] One important criterion for
judging the excellence of a particular work is its
successful or unsuccessful use of formulas and
formulaic systems and its use of the traditional
themes and type-scenes to produce a coherent,
aesthetically-pleasing poem which is unified and
consistent and has a meaningful system of imagery.
As we can see from the extant Old English poems,
a poet could manipulate formulaic half-lines to
produce a passage which expressed a particular idea
and became part of a unique system of subject-
matter and imagery within the poem. For example,
both Guthlac A and Guthlac B describe one of the
most commonplace events of hagiography, a scene in
which angels carry the saint's soul to Heaven, in
formulaic language; in fact, the passages are
introduced by variants of the same formulaic line.
The impacts of the passages differ because the two
poems emphasize different points. Guthlac A
describes man's exiled state and longing for a
secure homeland, and at the end, it shows that
Heaven is the only place where a person may be
"eardfæst"[13] (l. 786b) [secure in his home]:

        Swa wæs Guðlaces   gæst gelæded
        engla fæðmum   in uprodor
        fore onsyne   eces deman:
        læddon leoflice.   Him wæs lean geseald,

> setl on swegle, þær he symle mot
> awo to ealdre eardfæst wesan,
> bliðe bidan.
> (ll. 781a-87a)

[Thus Guthlac's spirit was brought in the
arms of the angels into the firmament
before the face of the Eternal Judge:
they brought it lovingly. A reward was
given to him, a seat in Heaven, where he
might always, forever, be secure in his
home, dwell happy].

In contrast, Guthlac B is concerned with the cycles
of Fall and Redemption and with the sorrows of
fallen man, and in the corresponding passage, it
emphasizes the transitoriness of earthly life and
the fate of Guthlac's body rather than the joys of
Heaven:

> Ða wæs Guðlaces gæst gelæded
> eadig on upweg; englas feredun
> to þam longan gefean; lic colode,
> belifd under lyfte.
> (ll. 1305a-8a)

[Then Guthlac's blessed spirit was brought
on the way to Heaven; angels bore it to
lasting joy; the body grew cold, deprived
of life under the sky.]

Scholars like Walter J. Ong and Alain Renoir
have shown that oral elements survive in works
which are undeniably the products of written traditions,[14] and we should therefore not be surprised
to find that they are present in the Guthlac poems
despite the fact that neither begins in a way
seemingly designed to attract the attention of an
audience and that both may have been composed in
writing. Moreover, both Guthlac A and B have been
influenced by Latin works, and the influences seem
to be of the type which can be explained only if
we believe that the authors had literary works
before them as they composed.[15] Guthlac A mentions

the "bec" (l. 528b) [books] that have taught us
about the miracles performed by Jesus, and <u>Guthlac
B</u> suggests that the audience as well as the author
is familiar with written works about Guthlac,
either by private reading or by listening to oral
presentations:[16]

                      Us secgað bec
        hu Guðlac wearð þurh Godes willan
        eadig on Engle.
                      (ll. 878b-80a)

[Books tell us how Guthlac was, by the
will of God, blessed among the English.]

However, both <u>Guthlac</u> <u>A</u> and <u>B</u> manipulate formulaic
elements as consciously as any oral poem does.

    Oral-formulaists have shown that an oral poet
composes his works within a context in which his
audience already knows the story and is interested
in assessing the merits of a particular performance.[17] As Fry points out, however, the audience
may also be familiar with a work from a literary
tradition and still want to hear new versions of
it recited. Speaking of <u>Judith</u>, he says, "If the
audience knew the story of Judith, as they most
certainly did, they would anticipate, on the basis
of their familiarity with the traditional themes,
the fulfilling of certain patterns as the tale
progressed . . . [and] would experience the
aesthetic pleasure inherent in the fulfillment of
familiar, anticipated patterns."[18] Like oral
poetry, hagiography is directed at an audience
which knows the story being related. Jones has
shown that hagiographies were often composed for
use in the liturgy celebrated on the feast-day of
the patron saint of a monastery and that an
audience would therefore hear the story of, for
example, St. Cuthbert, read "each year again come
Cuthbert's Day" (p. 73). As a result, a poet who
wished to compose a formulaic poem about St.
Cuthbert would have been composing for an audience
well-acquainted with his story. Similarly, the

Guthlac poems may have been composed for an audience which heard his story recounted every year on his feast-day, April 11, and perhaps on other occasions as well. In addition, the authors of both hagiographic narratives and oral-formulaic poetry are aware of the expectations of their audiences and try to fulfill them. Lord has shown that certain themes and formulas recur in every version of any particular tale,[19] and Jones comments that "in a saint's life the hero fails his audience as seldom as the hero of a modern romance with the count three and two in the ninth inning" (p. 73).

Many Old English poems repeat formulas in different contexts to explore various meanings of words or ideas. Daniel, for example, explores the related themes that wisdom and righteousness are the proper attributes of a godly man and that a perverted mind is characteristic of a Satanic person. It uses the word "mod" [the inner man; therefore, the mind, spirit, or heart] many times both as a simplex and as part of compound words and reiterates it in different contexts until we come to understand that there is a relationship between sanctity and man's mind and spiritual nature. The Israelites are described as a "modig cyn" (l. 7b) [noble-minded or wise people] before they rebel against God, forsake wisdom, and choose "deofles cræft" (l. 32b) [the devil's knowledge]. To punish them, God gives them into the power of the Babylonians whose lord, Nebuchadnezzar, is characterized by "swiðmod" (l. 100a) [harshness of mind] and tries to twist and pervert the minds of those Israelites who remain faithful to God.

Short passages within poems explore single words or images, as instanced by the last sixteen lines of Christ II which concentrate on the image of life as a journey over a cold ocean seeking the haven of salvation. Since man's need for salvation was the cause of Christ's Advent, these lines are intimately related to the main theme of the poem, the Ascension. The poem also describes Christ's

Passion, Resurrection, and Ascension through its exploration of an Old English poetic theme known as the "Cliff of Death," which describes a journey "niþer under næssas"[20] [down under the headlands] to death and Hell. In Christ II, Christ literally conquers the "Cliff of Death" by His Resurrection, for "godes ece bearn / ofer heahhleoþu hlypum stylde" (ll. 744b-45b) [God's eternal son sprang in leaps up over the high hills]. In "De Historiis Sanctorum," I have argued that the extant Old English hagiographic poems, Andreas, Juliana, Judith, Elene, and Guthlac, explore in depth themes that are brief, conventional episodes in Graeco-Latin works;[21] such exploration is similar to the way in which the poems discussed above explore words and ideas. The present study will examine the ways in which the Guthlac poems explore hagiographic commonplaces in heroic verse.

In order to appreciate fully the literary sophistication of the Guthlac poems, we must understand the proficiency with which the authors express their religious subject by heroic devices of composition. Only if we understand the ways in which they use the disparate traditions of Christian hagiography and Germanic heroic poetry will we be able to read the poems with a sympathetic understanding of both. Since the specialization of scholars today makes it unlikely that many will be attracted to both traditions, the Guthlac poems will undoubtedly--to borrow a line from Milton--"fit audience find, though few."[22]

Notes to Chapter One

[1] Some of the major works include Milman Parry's "Studies in the Epic Technique of Oral Verse-Making, I: Homer and Homeric Style," Harvard Studies in Classical Philology, 41 (1930), pp. 73-147 and "Studies in the Epic Technique of Oral Verse-Making, II: The Homeric Language as the Language of Oral Poetry," Harvard Studies in Classical Philology, 43 (1932), pp. 1-50; Albert B. Lord, The Singer of Tales, Harvard Studies in Comparative Literature, 24 (1960), rpt. New York: Atheneum, 1974; Francis P. Magoun, Jr., "Oral-Formulaic Character of Anglo-Saxon Narrative Poetry," Speculum, 28 (1953), pp. 446-67. All references to Lord's Singer of Tales appear in the text.

[2] F. H. Whitman, "The Meaning of 'Formulaic' in Old English Verse Composition," NM, 76 (1975), p. 529.

[3] Donald K. Fry, "Caedmon as a Formulaic Poet," Forum for Modern Language Studies, 10 (1974), p. 227.

[4] Edward B. Irving, Jr., "Image and Meaning in the Elegies," in Old English Poetry: Fifteen Essays, ed. Robert P. Creed (Providence, Rhode Island: Brown Univ. Press, 1967), p. 153. All further references appear in the text.

[5] Daniel G. Calder, "Guthlac A and Guthlac B: Some Discriminations," in Anglo-Saxon Poetry: Essays in Appreciation, for John C. McGalliard, ed. Lewis E. Nicholson and Dolores Warwick Frese (Notre Dame: Univ. of Notre Dame Press, 1975), p. 66.

[6] See, for example, Hippolyte Delehaye, Les Légendes Hagiographiques, 3rd. ed., Subsidia Hagiographica, vol. 18 (Bruxelles: Société des Bollandistes, 1927); Les Origines du Culte des

Martyrs, 2nd. ed., Subsidia Hagiographica, vol. 20 (Bruxelles: Société des Bollandistes, 1933); and Les Passions des Martyrs et les Genres Littéraires, 2nd. ed., Subsidia Hagiographica, vol. 13B (Bruxelles: Société des Bollandistes, 1966).

[7] See Charles W. Jones, Saints' Lives and Chronicles in Early England (Ithaca, New York: Cornell Univ. Press, 1947) and Robert W. Hanning, The Vision of History in Early Britain: From Gildas to Geoffrey of Monmouth (New York: Columbia Univ. Press, 1966). All references to Jones's Saints' Lives appear in the text.

[8] Alexandra Hennessey Olsen, "'De Historiis Sanctorum': A Generic Study of Hagiography," Genre, 13 (1980), 407-29.

[9] Michael D. Cherniss, Ingeld and Christ: Heroic Concepts and Values in Old English Christian Poetry (The Hague: Mouton, 1972), p. 219. All further references appear in the text.

[10] Clinton J. Albertson, S. J., Anglo-Saxon Saints and Heroes (New York: Fordham Univ. Press, 1967), p. 25. All further references appear in the text.

[11] Rosemary Woolf, "Saints' Lives," Continuations and Beginnings: Studies in Old English Literature, ed. Eric Gerald Stanley (London: Thomas Nelson and Sons, Ltd., 1966), p. 39. All further references appear in the text.

[12] Edward M. Palumbo's The Literary Use of Formulas in Guthlac II and Their Relation to Felix's Vita Sancti Guthlaci (The Hague and Paris: Mouton, 1977) denies the validity of formulaic analysis of Old English poetry because Palumbo equates formularity with orality. The most recent work on the subject which he cites is Ann Chalmers Watts's The Lyre and the Harp, A Comparative Reconsideration of Oral Tradition in Homer and Old English Epic Poetry (New Haven: Yale Univ. Press, 1969),

and he does not refer to such important articles as Fry's "Caedmon as a Formulaic Poet." Because Palumbo is concerned only with showing that Guthlac B could not have been composed orally--a fact on which scholars agree--his work is of no critical use to the modern student of Guthlac B.

[13] Quotations from Guthlac are from The Guthlac Poems of the Exeter Book, ed. Jane Roberts (Oxford: Clarendon Press, 1979) and are quoted by permission of Oxford Univ. Press. Quotations from Beowulf are from Beowulf and the Fight at Finnsburg, ed. Friedrich Klaeber, 3rd. ed. with 1st. and 2nd. Supplements (Boston: D. C. Heath and Co., 1950). Quotations from The Phoenix are from The Phoenix, ed. N. F. Blake (Manchester: Manchester Univ. Press, 1964). Quotations from the other Old English poems are from the Anglo-Saxon Poetic Records, ed. George Philip Krapp and Elliott Van Kirk Dobbie, 6 vols. (New York: Columbia Univ. Press, 1931, 1932, 1936, 1953, 1932, and 1942; rpt. 1969). All references appear in the text.

[14] See Walter J. Ong, S. J., "Oral Residue in Tudor Prose Style," Rhetoric, Romance and Technology: Studies in the Interaction of Expression and Culture (Ithaca and London: Cornell Univ. Press, 1971), pp. 23-47; Alain Renoir, "Oral-Formulaic Theme Survival: A Possible Instance in the 'Nibelungenlied'," NM, 65 (1964), pp. 70-75.

[15] For example, Thomas D. Hill argues in "The Typology of the Week and the Numerical Structure of the Old English Guthlac B," MS, 37 (1975), "that the Guthlac B poet was aware of the traditional typology of the week, and that this tradition is relevant for the formal structure of the poem" (p. 532) and that the poet's work shows "intellectual sophistication" (p. 536) because of its numerical structure.

[16] In A Concordance to The Anglo-Saxon Poetic Records (Ithaca and London: Cornell Univ. Press, 1978), p. 105, J. B. Bessinger, Jr., lists eight

formulaic half-lines which say "books tell us," although the verbs cyðað and cweðaþ are used as well as the more common secgað (six occurrences). In addition, the line, "Hwæt, we þæt hyrdon þurh halige bec" occurs four times in works by Cynewulf. Most of the poems which use such lines have written sources: Genesis A, The Fates of the Apostles, Elene, Christ II, Guthlac B, and The Lord's Prayer II; the formula also occurs in a poem composed in the latter portion of the Old English period, The Battle of Brunanburh. The use of the formula resembles Ælfric's use of similar statements to link his homilies to the preceding biblical readings. For example, he begins the Sermo de Die Iudicii with the words, "Seo halige Cristes boc þe ymbe Cristes wundra sprycð / segð . . ." [Homilies of Ælfric: A Supplementary Collection, vol. 2, ed. John C. Pope, EETS, Old Series vol. 260 (London, New York, and Toronto: The Early English Text Society, 1968), p. 590].

[17] Students of living oral traditions speak about the existence of "a diverse, and sometimes large, actively participating audience" and about the fact that the singer "creates while he performs. He selects, adjusts, and modifies episodes, sometimes in response to the actual composition of his audience or in response to the social position of his hosts and sponsors" [Daniel P. Biebuyck, "The African Heroic Epic," Heroic Epic and Saga: An Introduction to the World's Great Folk Epics, ed. Felix J. Oinas (Bloomington and London: Indiana Univ. Press, 1978), pp. 351 and 350]. Jeff Opland has recently reiterated that "audience and oral performer participate in a social activity" [Anglo-Saxon Oral Poetry: A Study of the Traditions (New Haven and London: Yale Univ. Press, 1980), p. 80].

[18] Fry, "The Heroine on the Beach in Judith," NM, 68 (1967), pp. 181-82.

[19] See Lord, Singer of Tales, pp. 242-65, for a discussion of the recurrence of formulaic elements

in the Yugoslavian tales about the Return of the Hero.

[20]"The Cliff of Death" has been discussed by Fry in an unpublished article, "The Cliff of Death in Old English Poetry," presented at the 1980 meeting of the MLA. The formulaic expression "niþer under næssas" occurs, for example, in Guthlac, l. 563a, and Christ and Satan, l. 90a.

[21]Olsen, "De Historiis Sanctorum." In the article, I mention in passing some of the ideas developed in this study.

[22]John Milton, Paradise Lost, Bk. VII, l. 31, Complete Poems and Major Prose, ed. Merritt Y. Hughes (New York: The Odyssey Press, 1957). All further references appear in the text.

Chapter Two
The Return of the Hero-Saint:
A Reconsideration of Guthlac A

Section A
Homily and Hagiography:
The Learned Background

Guthlac A has often been viewed as "eine Heiligenpredigt im Gewande altenglischer Dichtungssprache"[1] and has usually received less-than-favorable criticism. Some scholars criticize it for being homiletic and agree with Woolf that as a literary work it is "limited and inflexible" (p. 57). Those who praise the homiletic qualities of Guthlac A often seem relatively unconcerned with the question of whether or not the versified homily is a successful literary work. Lawrence K. Shook, for example, says that "it is scarcely unfair to the poem to describe it as a kind of theological treatise on angels," and he dismisses the heroic language and formulas of the poem as having merely "a surface resemblance"[2] to those of Old English heroic poetry. Even Frances Randall Lipp, who praises "the poet's skilled and resourceful adaptation of literary conventions,"[3] criticizes "the poem's overt and obtrusive didacticism" (p. 59) and concludes that "its didactic approach puts it in a tradition of popular preaching and suggests that the poet had the needs of an unsophisticated audience in mind" (p. 62). The implications of this assumption seem to be that homilies can appeal only to the unsophisticated and that therefore the original audience of Guthlac A must have lacked sophistication. I submit that such implications are unwarranted, given the nature of medieval homilies and hagiographic narratives and of the probable audiences of Old English poetry.

Virtually all hagiographies, including acknowledged literary masterpieces written for sophisticated audiences, have a homiletic stance similar to that of Guthlac A, which at one point interjects

an assurance of the veracity of the story into
the middle of the narrative and by so doing makes
us, the poem's audience, the witnesses who can
guarantee the truth of the story: "Hwæt we þissa
wundra gewitan sindon" (l. 752) [Lo, we are witnesses of these miracles]. As Jones points out,
hagiographic works usually cite "authorities . . .
[who can] testify that the implications of . . .
[the story are] in the saintly pattern" (pp. 75-
76). He shows that even Bede's Vita Cuthberti,
generally acknowledged to be one of the literary
masterpieces of the Anglo-Saxon period, "cites
authority for most miracles" (p. 75) related.
After recounting one miracle, for example, Bede
states, "Ut frater quidam nostri monasterii proba-
tissimus cuius ipse haec relatione didici, sese
haec ab uno ipsorum rusticae simplicitatis uiro,
et simulandi prorsus ignaro, coram multis sepe
assidentibus audisse narrauerit"[4] [In fact a very
worthy brother of our monastery, from whose lips
I heard the story, declared that he himself had
often heard these things related in the presence
of many by one of these same people, a man of
rustic simplicity and absolutely incapable of in-
venting an untruth]. Far from being intended for
an unsophisticated audience, Bede's Vita Cuthberti
addressed itself "domino sancto ac beatissimo
patri Eadfrido episcopo, sed et omni congregationi
fratrum qui in Lindisfarnensi insula Christo
deseruiunt" (pp. 142-43) [to the holy and most
blessed father, Bishop Eadfrith, and also to the
whole congregation of brethren who serve Christ on
the island of Lindisfarne]. Lindisfarne was a
major center of learning, and it is reasonable
to assume that the educated audience of Bede's
Latin hagiography also appreciated those vernacular versions which are found in monastic manuscripts, especially since the Latin and vernacular
works share a similar didactic purpose.

Unlike Bede's works but like those of Ælfric
and Wulfstan, Guthlac A is in English. The language does not indicate the intended audience of
the poem, for Latin works like Bede's Historia

Ecclesiastica and Felix's Vita Guthlaci were dedicated to prominent laymen and seem accordingly to have been composed for lay audiences. Jones believes that Felix must have been writing for laymen because "he expands his tale with panegyric . . . [and] with references to time and place. . . . He tends to neglect the stock formulas about witnesses in favor of an overall reference in the Preface. And he not only dedicates his narrative to one King, but makes another King its juvenile lead. In these few characteristics we see the pressure to secularize the form. There are other suggestions of a lay audience: . . . [the] clear picture of Bishop Haedde and his company, the accent on Guthlac's noble lineage . . . and the comparative disregard of cloister life" (p. 86). Similarly, vernacular works were used in monasteries;[5] indeed, all extant Old English poetry is found in monastic manuscripts, accompanied by religious works. George Herzfeld, the modern editor of the Old English Martyrology, points out that the evidence suggests that this vernacular work was composed to be related to "a monastic audience . . . [at] a service in a place where laymen would not be present."[6] Two poems, A Summons to Prayer and The Phoenix, contain alternate Old English and Latin half-lines, and Aldhelm consists of a mixture of Latin, Greek, and Old English. Such macaronic poems could only be meaningful to an audience able to understand classical languages and are therefore probably monastic, but they are also obviously directed at an audience which appreciated poems written in the vernacular. In addition, the fact that all extant vernacular poetry is found in monastic manuscripts suggests that the learned writers of the scriptoria liked such poetry, an important fact since only monastic manuscripts had a chance to survive. Woolf comments that the existence of the hagiographic poems tells us nothing about their original audience except that it liked heroic poetry: "The verse lives, whether intended for a lay or ecclesiastical audience, were obviously primarily intended as edifying substitutes for heroic poetry, . . . and they could be best appreciated by those familiar with Old English heroic literature" (p. 39). Moreover, in view of the fact that, as Woolf points out, it was not until "the late tenth century [that] hagiography became a part of the remarkable movement to provide sermons in the vernacular for the common people" (p. 39), it seems extremely unlikely that Guthlac A was intended for what Lipp calls an "unsophisticated audience" (p. 62).

In contrast to Lipp, some scholars have argued that Guthlac A is aimed at a sophisticated audience. Fred C. Robinson, for example, suggests that the poet expected his audience to be familiar with Latin interpretations of Biblical names, for he "inserts a learned interpretation of the name Hierusalem into his closing sentence"[7] and introduces Guthlac's patron saint Bartholomew not by name but by "the curious hapax legomenon ofermæcg" (p. 168). Robinson notes that "the literal meaning of the compound would seem to be 'the man above' or 'the son from above' . . . [and that] the name Bartholomaeus is explicated by the commentators constantly and consistently as meaning, etymologically, filius suspendentis aquas" (pp. 168-69). However, in the poetic works of Sedulius Scotus, "the original etymology is . . . reduced to filius 'son' and celsus 'above'; that is, to almost precise equivalents of the OE epithet ofermæcg" (p. 169), a fact that could only be appreciated by an educated audience. Furthermore, Guthlac A resembles other Old English poems that must have appealed to educated audiences. The highly literary and theological Dream of the Rood has homiletic qualities similar to those of Guthlac A that make its place among the homilies of the Vercelli Book appropriate. The Dream of the Rood is undoubtedly a better poem than is Guthlac A, but nevertheless it begins in a homiletic style:

    Hwæt! Ic swefna cyst secgan wylle,
   hwæt me gemætte to midre nihte,
  syðþan reordberend reste wunedon!
           (ll. 1a-3b)

> [Lo! I will tell you the best of dreams,
> what I dreamed in the middle of the night,
> while speech-bearers stayed in bed.]

The beginning of the Dream of the Rood resembles that of Beowulf, which uses a formula intended to catch the attention of an audience:

> Hwæt, we Gar-Dena   in geardagum,
> þeodcyninga   þrym gefrunon,
> hu ða æþelingas   ellen fremedon!
> (ll. 1a-3b)

> [Lo, we have heard of the glory of the
> Spear-Danes, of the kings of the people,
> in days of yore, how the noblemen per-
> formed deeds of valor!]

Guthlac A uses similar formulaic lines, although not to begin the narrative; instead, it uses them to introduce homiletic digressions. One important digression occurs when the poet wonders about the paradox of the Crucifixion:

>   Hwæt þæt wundra sum
> monnum þuhte   þæt he ma wolde
> afrum onfengum   earme gæstas
> hrinan leton,   7 þæt hwæþre gelomp.
> (ll. 517b-20b)

> [Lo, that seems a particular wonder to men,
> that He would let the wretched spirits
> touch him more with their fierce grasps,
> and that nevertheless came to pass.]

The homiletic digressions therefore place Guthlac A in the mainstream of both the hagiographic and the Old English poetic traditions. In addition, they provide a balance to the narrative passages, reinforcing the themes presented therein. The passages in Guthlac A which precede the homiletic digression about the Crucifixion explore the nature of life and death, describe the diabolic persecution of Guthlac, and show that Guthlac is

living a life appropriate for a righteous person.
The digression states explicitly that his life is
ruled by God and emphasizes that even his torments
are permitted by God. Guthlac has repeatedly said
that he trusts in God, and at this point he avers,
"Ic gebidan wille / þæs þe min dryhten demeð" (ll.
378b-79a) [I will endure whatever my Lord ad-
judges to me]. In so doing, he echoes the prayer
of Christ before His Passion, "Veruntamen non mea
voluntas, sed tua fiat"[8] (Luke 22:42) [May Thy
will, not Mine, be done]. The homiletic passage
shows that, by accepting God's will, Guthlac resembles Christ, Who patiently endured "ehtendra nið"
(l. 525b) [the hatred of persecutors].

In addition to being aimed at a learned audience, Guthlac A seems to have been written for a
monastic one. Cynthia Edelstein Cornell has suggested that the poet organized and developed Guthlac A according to the "ruminative mode of composition"[9] used in the monasteries, a mode "fostered
by the monastic practice of meditation upon Scrip-
ture" (p. 190). Zacharias P. Thundyil views Guthlac A as a poem about and influenced specifically
by Benedictine monasticism. He points out that
"for the Anglo-Saxons of the Benedictine tradition
. . . their whole life was a spiritual warfare,
one in which Christ was the king, and the monk his
soldier. The monastic rule was the strict military code under which this soldier served."[10]
Thundyil maintains that Guthlac A owes many of its
conceptions and images to St. Benedict's Regula
Monachorum. In an unpublished paper, Thomas R.
Post has suggested that "there is more than a
casual alliance between Guthlac A and the writings
of St. Benedict. . . . It is probable, moreover,
based on the evidence of dictional similarities,
that the author of Guthlac A had a manuscript of
the Regula available to him."[11] One purpose of
the author of Guthlac A may have been similiar to
that of Bishop Æthelwold, who translated the
Regula during the tenth century: to make the
ideas of St. Benedict available in English.

Many of the themes and incidents in Guthlac A show that the poem was intended for an educated, monastic audience. Guthlac is the perfect--indeed, one might say the archetypal--hermit who lives in the era of Grace initiated by Christ's Advent. He raises "Cristes rode" (l. 180a) [the Cross of Christ] in the wasteland, and afterwards the devils "singales sorge dreogað" (l. 219) [always endure sorrow]. Guthlac brings sorrow to the devils of the wasteland by his arrival there, just as Christ's Advent defeated the Devil. Luke recounts how one devil recognized Jesus as the destroyer who had come to disturb his peace and called out, "Sine, quid nobis et tibi, Iesu Nazarene? venisti perdere nos? scio te quis sis, Sanctus Dei" (Luke 4:34-35) [What do you want with us, Jesus the Nazarene? Have you come to destroy us? I know who you are, the Holy One of God]. The devils of Guthlac A are no longer able "on eorþan eardes brucan" (l. 220) [to enjoy a home on earth], and they are condemned to eternal suffering. They wish "þæt him dryhten þurh deaðes cwealm / to hyra earfeða ende geryme" (ll. 224a-25b) [that the Lord would put an end to their miseries by the destruction of death], although the end will never come. The eternal sorrow of the devils is so fundamental a Christian point that it could hardly have failed to evoke a response from the audience of Guthlac A. It is described in many literary works, including such major English poems as Genesis B and Paradise Lost. Genesis B reiterates several times that Satan is he who "helle forð healdan sceolde, / gieman þæs grundes" (ll. 348a-49a) [must henceforth hold Hell, take care of the abyss] and that in Hell he and his followers "wite þolien, / hearm" (ll. 367b-68a) [suffer torment and pain], while Paradise Lost states that the Devil is "confounded though immortal" (Bk. I, l. 53).

Although some modern critics have been concerned with discussing the original audience of Guthlac A and the homiletic qualities of the poem, others have focused on discussions which concern the integrity of the manuscript of the poem. They argue that the first twenty-nine lines of Guthlac A were placed at the beginning of the poem by a scribal error and must either form the conclusion of the preceding poem in the manuscript, Christ III, or belong to a completely separate poem which the compiler of the Exeter Book put in its present location because it was "a fragment for which he wanted to find a place."[12] George Philip Krapp and Elliott Van Kirk Dobbie, for example, state that the lines are "only very remotely connected with the narrative of the life of Guthlac which begins with Monge sindon."[13] In Anglo-Saxon Poetry, R. K. Gordon translates the lines as the conclusion of Christ III and begins Guthlac A at line 30,[14] and he does not consider the re-arrangement of the lines as they appear in the manuscript important enough to warrant a footnote. In contrast, other critics believe that these twenty-nine lines contain key words and themes which are developed later in the poem.[15] I find myself in agreement with the latter view, especially since arguments for removing the lines are usually based on misunderstandings about the poem. In addition, since we have only one extant manuscript of Guthlac, since that manuscript seems to indicate that the scribe considered the lines to be an integral part of Guthlac,[16] and since there is no overwhelming evidence to support their deletion, purely pragmatic considerations prompt us to respect the manuscript's integrity and consider those lines the beginning of our extant Guthlac A. Furthermore, from the point of view of the student of the contents and structure of the poem, the question of authorial unity is irrelevant, for the poem as it appears in the manuscript is a unified work.

Calder has pointed out that even critics who believe that the prologue is part of Guthlac A have often expressed "an uneasiness" with its "rhetorical and logical structure."[17] Such uneasiness is, however, unwarranted, for the prologue is thematically linked to the rest of the poem. Guthlac A explores at length the subject of the joys of the Redemption announced in its first line:

"Se bið gefeana fægrast þonne hy æt frymðe gemetað, / engel 7 seo eadge sawl" (ll. 1a-2a) [That is the fairest of joys when they first meet, the angel and the blessed soul]. Just as <u>Guthlac A</u> begins with a description of joy, so it ends with the word "wynne" (l. 818b) [pleasure or joy] and emphasizes the "sibbe" (l. 816a) [peace] that the redeemed experience, "wynnum" (l. 814b) [joyfully] and "georne" (l. 815b) [eagerly], in Heaven.

<u>Guthlac A</u> contrasts transitory earthly joy and eternal heavenly joy, and the redeemed soul of the prologue leaves "þas lænan dreamas" (l. 3a) [the transitory joys] for those of Heaven. Guthlac points out that "God scop geoguðe 7 gumena dream" (l. 495) [God created youth and the joy of men], and he suggests that a man's love of earthly joys can be transformed into a love of heavenly joy:

> Ne magun þa æfteryld in þam ærestan
> blæde geberan ac hy blissiað
> worulde wynnum oððæt wintra rim
> gegæð in þa geoguðe þæt se gæst lufað
> onsyn 7 ætwist yldran hades
> ðe gemete monige geond middangeard
> þeowiað in þeawum.
>   (ll. 496a-502a)

> [They (young men) may not show maturity in their first bloom, but they delight in the joys of the world, until a number of winters come upon their youth, so that the spirit loves the appearance and form of the elder state, which in a seemly way many throughout the world serve in their customs.]

The theme that the love of earthly things can lead to the love of heavenly things has persisted throughout the Christian period. Sulpicius Severus, for example, exhibited it in his own life when, after the loss of his beloved wife, he "retired from the world . . . lived a life of semi-

seclusion under the direction of St. Martin . . .
[and was] ordained."[18] Even during the Renaissance,
Edmund Spenser can turn to the theme to prove that
heavenly things are more important than earthly;
in the incomplete eighth canto of the Seventh Book
of The Faerie Queene, he comments that he has come
to "loath this state of life so tickle"[19] and love
Heaven instead. Guthlac A's emphasis on joy and
on the contrast between earthly and heavenly joys
would be less striking without the prologue which
introduces the theme.

The prologue introduces two other important
themes. One is that of "had"[20] (l. 4b), a word
which, as Calder points out, "appears four more
times within the opening 94 lines, that is, within
the 92-line general introduction and the first two
lines of the narrative proper. This fairly
striking example of 'clustered repetition' . . .
establishes some concerns that occupy the poet."[21]
The other theme is that of exile, introduced in
the third line, which commends the soul's voluntary
abandonment of "lænan dreamas" (l. 3a) [transitory
joys], and brought up again when Guthlac and the
devils discuss the question of who is an exile and
who is not.

Since the first four lines of the prologue
introduce three important themes developed in the
poem, we have pragmatic reasons to assume that the
prologue is indeed part of Guthlac A. We may,
therefore, comply with Benjamin K. Thorpe's
admonition, in the introduction to the facsimile
edition of the Exeter Book, that we "follow the
scribe in regarding the twenty-nine lines . . . as
the prologue to Guthlac A."[22]

Section B
Formula and Theme:
The Heroic Background

Because of its homiletic nature, Guthlac A
has often been subjected to criticism which fails
to discuss the merits of the poem. George K.
Anderson, for example, has said that "Guthlac A has
little to recommend it to anyone other than the
antiquarian and student of Old English language and
poetry,"[23] and so perceptive a scholar as Woolf has
criticized it as "shapeless because there is no
story to progress" and says that "its lack of
variety in content is reflected in monotony of tone,
which is didactic and narrowly heroic, unvaried and
unsubtle" (pp. 56-57). Even some critics who like
the poem precisely because it is homiletic assume
that it has little literary value.

The theological and monastic themes of Guthlac
A are undeniably important, and Shook has even
stated that "the heart of Guthlac A is to be found
beating in the religious and theological notions
which the protagonists debate or which the narrator
dwells upon."[24] Nevertheless, we must be careful
not to ignore the importance of the form and language of the poem, especially since Guthlac A
contains numerous passages which remind the modern
reader of passages of heroic poetry and which must
have made an even greater impression on the
original Anglo-Saxon audience. In his study of the
heroic language used in Old English Christian
poetry, Cherniss has shown that the language plays
an integral part in the poetry. He suggests that
although "Christian spiritual ideals control the
narrative [of Guthlac A], . . . the poet . . .
[employs] heroic concepts . . . as metaphors to
describe the extra-terrestrial, spiritual world of
Christianity" (p. 226), and his examination of
the heroic vocabulary and imagery shows that
Guthlac A's poetic beauty is greatly enhanced by
their presence. I should like to argue, however,
that the heroic vocabulary of Guthlac A is not

merely metaphorical, for the poet has transferred the language from a description of secular heroism to one of religious heroism. It seems likely that the poem was composed for a sophisticated, monastic audience, capable both of understanding learned allusions and theological speculations and of appreciating Old English heroic poetry. Thus, if Guthlac A is a successful literary work, it must be successful, not only as a versified, homiletic call to the monastic life, but also as a formulaic Old English poem.

Many Old English poems appear static to a modern audience because they develop by repetition and balance rather than by presenting a sequential narrative. Guthlac A is such a poem, "circular in its structure [and] ritual in its action."[25] Beowulf itself, the only long heroic poem which has survived from the Old English period and which may even have originally been composed orally,[26] has a similar structure. Scholars have frequently debated the question of the unity of Beowulf, for like Guthlac, Beowulf shows repetition of plot and event. J. R. R. Tolkien suggests that Beowulf neither "tells a tale . . . [nor] intends to tell a tale sequentially. . . . It is essentially a balance, an opposition of ends and beginnings . . . [and has a] simple and static structure."[27] Likewise, Joan Blomfield has pointed out that "the setting out of the material is not in Beowulf an evolution, following one main line or connecting thread. Instead, the subject is disposed as a circumscribed field in which the themes are drawn out by a centre of attraction--in this case, the character of the good warrior."[28] In a recent study, Renoir has reiterated the fact that Beowulf has a static nature and points out as well that most "of the poem repeatedly plays upon our sense of time by intermingling past, future, and present, as when both Beowulf's past exploits and the future catastrophes resultant from his death are brought to bear upon his present sacrifice to impress us with the tragic dignity of the event."[29]

Other Old English poems also have static structures and describe events without reference to a strict chronological sequence. Christ and Satan, for example, describes the history of the world from Creation to Judgment Day but intermingles episodes in such a way that it eliminates the linear dimension of history. As a result, the poem provides a perspective on history which permits us to understand the close relationships between such events as Fall and Redemption and the first and second Advents of Christ. In addition, the poem begins and ends with descriptions of the Fallen Angels lamenting in Hell but moves to both Heaven and Earth in its middle portion, and it emphasizes that Heaven, Hell, and Earth are mutually exclusive. The structure of Christ and Satan is static, and the poem does not advance as a linear narrative but instead balances the lamenting angels at beginning and end, the events of Fall and Redemption, and the joy of the angels and redeemed mankind against the misery of the devils.

Like such poems, Guthlac A does not develop as a linear narrative; instead, it consists of series of repeated incidents. One of the series presents one of the most important themes of the poem, the existence of good and evil spirits who try to possess the souls of men. In the prologue, Guthlac A speaks about "gefeana fægrast" (l. la) [the fairest of joys] experienced by the good spirits when a human soul goes to Heaven. Those who go to Heaven are those who during their lives "Cristes æ / lærað 7 læstað 7 his lof rærað" (ll. 23b-24b) [teach and follow the law of Christ and raise up His praise] and who in addition "oferwinnað þa awyrgdan gæstas" (l. 25a) [vanquish the accursed spirits]. The first lines of the prologue of Guthlac A thus introduce the themes of the conflict between good and evil spirits and of the necessity for a good man to overcome the evil ones. A few lines later, Guthlac A shows the conflict between good and evil spirits for the souls of the hermits, who are persecuted by the devils because of their great holiness:

>   Oft him brogan to
> laðne gelædeð   se þe him lifes ofonn,
> eaweð him egsan, hwilum idel wuldor,
> brægdwis bona, --hafað bega cræft--
> eahteð anbuendra.
>   (ll. 84b-88a)

[Often he who begrudges them life brings
hostility as a horror against them, shows
them terror and, at times, empty glory; the
crafty slayer--he has power over both--
terrifies lone-dwellers.]

Although hermits are persecuted by the Devil and
his hosts, they are protected by angels "gearwe
mid gæsta wæpnum" (l. 89a) [ready with the weapons
of spirits]. After this general statement about
the existence of warfare between angels and devils,
Guthlac A turns to the specific case of Guthlac,
describing the past struggle between angels and
devils for the soul of a holy Englishman who, as
we who know his story are aware, went to Heaven,
"þær he symle mot / awo to ealdre eardfæst wesan"
(ll. 785b-86b) [where he might always, forever,
be secure in his home]. Because both the poet and
his audience are aware that Guthlac's story ended
in the same way as that of the generalized "eadge
sawl" (l. 2a) [blessed soul] of the prologue,
there is no need for the poem to develop dramati-
cally. Instead, its emphasis is on the fact that
good and evil might balance each other were it not
for the miraculous intervention of God in human
affairs.

Guthlac's life is watched over by two guardians, "engel dryhtnes 7 se atela gæst" (l. 116)
[the angel of the Lord and the dreadful spirit],
each of whom urges Guthlac to follow his counsel.[30]
The two spirits are evenly balanced in this combat,
and neither of them is able to win control of
Guthlac "oþþæt þæs gewinnes weoroda dryhten / on
þæs engles dom ende gereahte" (ll. 134a-35b)

[until the Lord of Hosts decided the end of the combat in accordance with the will of the angel]. Although the battle between the guardian spirits has been decided "on þæs engles dom," and although "fæle freoðuweard" (l. 173a) [a faithful guardian of peace] is near Guthlac while he lives in his hermitage, he is continuously persecuted by the devils. The attacks follow the pattern established by the battle of the good and evil angels: first the devils attack, then Guthlac, assisted by the "frofre gæst" (l. 136b) [spirit of consolation], puts them to flight, and finally God decides the outcome of the conflict by sending St. Bartholomew to assist Guthlac. The repeated incidents in Beowulf likewise give an air of stasis and repetitiveness to the poem. Beowulf not only kills Grendel's dam but also reports to Hrothgar about the deed, and after he returns to Hygelac's court, he reports twice to his lord. Thus, we as audience perceive the same event four times from slightly different points of view.

Guthlac A balances images as well as themes in a static pattern. At one point, the devils attempt to make Guthlac as miserable as they themselves are by speaking "sarstafum" (l. 234a) [with bitter words] and threatening "þæt he deaþa gedal dreogan sceolde" (l. 235) [that he should endure the allotment of death]. Guthlac, however, knows that they are powerless either to end their own miseries or to slay him, and he tells them, "Þeah þe ge me deað gehaten, / mec wile wið þam niþum genergan se þe eowrum nydum wealdeð" (ll. 240b-41b) [Although you promise me death, He Who rules your distresses will preserve me from that hostility]. Guthlac A balances the miseries of the devils with its descriptions of joy. Furthermore, it mentions two kinds of joy which balance each other, the "lænan dreamas" (l. 3a) [transitory joys] of earth and the eternal joys of Heaven. Guthlac A's prologue contrasts those who value "eorðwela" (l. 62a) [earthly riches] and those who value "ece lif / hyhta hyhst" (ll. 62b-63a) [eternal life, the highest of joys]. In the

middle of the poem, the devils tempt Guthlac to
despair by showing him a vision of monks who value
the former although their vocation should inspire
them to value the latter:

> Sealdon him meahte   ofer monna cynn
> þæt he fore eagum   eall sceawode
> under haligra   hyrda gewealdum
> in mynsterum   monna gebæru
> þara þe hyra lifes   þurh lust brucan
> idlum æhtum   7 oferwlencum.
>   (ll. 413a-18b)

> [They gave him power greater than that of
> mankind, so that he beheld before his eyes
> all the behavior of the men in monasteries
> under the authority of holy shepherds, of
> those who spend their lives in pleasure,
> with idle possessions and ostentation.]

Guthlac A presents earthly life as the pivot point
between eternal joy and sorrow, for one may choose
to value "eorðwela" and doom himself to an eternity
of diabolic misery or to value "ece lif" and have
an eternity of joy.

The theme of joy is closely linked to that of
"had" (l. 4b) [person, rank, or the monastic
vocation]. Just as Daniel explores the multiple
meanings of "mod," so Guthlac A explores those of
"had" and uses it with several different meanings.
Calder analyzes Guthlac A's use of the term "had,"
which he translates as meaning both "person" and
"rank," and concludes that "the poet often plays
with the double meaning" of the term to establish
his "dominant themes: the hierarchical order of
the world, the necessity for obedience, and the
positive force of God's love that makes salvation
possible for holy men of all ranks."[31] Guthlac A
also plays with another meaning of the term,[32] for
"had" often refers specifically to the monastic
vocation. The Pœnitentiale Ecgberti Archepiscopi
Eboracensis, for example, uses the phrase "to hade
fon"[33] to mean "to take orders," and Wulfstan

speaks of "hadbrycas"[34] [injuries done to persons in holy orders] as one of the sins for which the eleventh-century English are being punished by God. Guthlac A emphasizes the importance of obedience and discipline in a Christian life and develops the theme of "had" by describing the life and apotheosis of a holy hermit.

Many Old English poems manipulate the sympathies of the audience, as for example Beowulf does, making us perceive Grendel's mother as a mother mourning for her dead son and therefore justified in pursuing a blood feud for him:

> Þæt gesyne wearþ,
> widcuþ werum, þætte wrecend þa gyt
> lifde æfter laþum, lange þrage,
> æfter guðceare; Grendles modor,
> ides aglæcwif yrmþe gemunde.
> . . . .
> . . . . . . His modor þa gyt
> gifre ond galgmod gegan wolde
> sorhfulne siþ, sunu deoð wrecan.
> (ll. 1255b-78b)

[It was seen and widely known by men that an avenger still lived for a long time after the hostile one, after the sorrow of battle: Grendel's mother, a female "aglæca," mindful of her misery. Then his mother still, greedy and sad in mind, wished to go on a sorrowful journey, to avenge the death of her son.]

The description of Grendel's mother and her desire to avenge her son follows the descriptions of how Hildeburh lost her son in battle against her brothers and committed him to the flames "æt Hnæfes ade" (l. 1114b) [on the pyre of Hnæf] and of how Wealtheo worries about the safety of her "byre" (l. 1188b) [sons (perceived from the mother's point of view)] if "wine Scildinga worold oflæt[eð]" (l. 1183) [the Lord of the Scyldings leaves the world]. Beowulf describes three sorrowing mothers and so gives us the point of view of the "aglæcwif" before describing her effect on the men with whom we normally sympathize.

Beowulf's use of the term "aglæca"[35] [miserable being, monster, wretch] also manipulates our sympathies because the term describes both men and monsters. For example, the poem calls Sigemund an "aglæca" (l. 893a) when he kills a "wrætlicne wyrm" (l. 891a) [splendid dragon] so that "he beahhordes brucan moste / selfes dome" (ll. 894a-95a) [he might enjoy the ring-hoard according to his own judgment]. Marion Lois Huffines has suggested that the term "aglæca" is associated with a being who possesses magical powers, but that "this magic is also associated with a moral decline on the part of monsters and heroes: monsters ravage and plunder in the domain of men, men do likewise in the monster's domain."[36] Although Guthlac resembles the "aglæcas" Sigemund and Beowulf by "ravaging" in the "domain" of the devils, Guthlac A uses the word only to refer to the devils, the "earme aglæcan" (l. 575a) [wretched "aglæcas"].

Beowulf makes us feel sympathy for the villains of the poem, describing Grendel's death in lines which have overtones of pity because they make Grendel seem like human beings:

> No þæt yðe byð
> to befleonne --fremme se þe wille--
> ac gesecan sceal sawlberendra
> nyde genydde, niþða bearna,
> grundbuendra gearwe stowe,
> þær his lichoma legerbedde fæst
> swefeþ æfter symle.
> (ll. 1002b-8a)

[Nor is it [death] easy to flee from--let him try who wants to--but he must seek the prepared place, ordained by fate for the soul-bearers, the children of men, the earth-dwellers, where his body, fast on the bed of death, sleeps after the feast.]

In an analogous way, Guthlac A manipulates our sympathies when Guthlac occupies the territory of the devils. He establishes his hermitage in a "dygle stow . . . / idel 7 æmen" (ll. 215a-16a) [secret spot, empty and uninhabited] which the devils have been able "æfter tintergum tidum brucan / ðonne hy of waþum werge cwoman" (ll. 211a-12b) [to enjoy at times after their torments when they have come weary from their wanderings]. Guthlac A makes us feel pity for the "earme ondsacan" (l. 210a) [wretched adversaries] who have been deprived of their last refuge, especially when they accuse Guthlac of being a sinful man who "for wlence on westenne / beorgas bræce" (ll. 208a-9a) [broke into the barrows in the waste because of pride]. Guthlac's invasion of the devils' refuge in the fens of Croyland reminds us of that of the "niðða nathwylc" (l. 2215a) [certain man] of Beowulf who invades the dragon's "stanbeorh" (l. 2213a) [rocky barrow], steals a flagon, and causes the dragon to begin a feud with the Geats. It is interesting to note that Felix's Vita itself describes an analogous incident, for it mentions the fact that Guthlac builds his hermitage on "tumulus agrestibus glaebis coacervatus, quem olim avari solitudinis frequentatores lucri ergo illic adquirendi defodientes scindebant" (pp. 92 and 94) [a mound piled up with clods of earth, which former avaricious frequenters of the waste had dug open, hoping thereby to acquire treasure]. The act of building a hermitage thus resembles the actions of evil men, but it is done for a just reason.

Like the dragons slain by Sigemund and Beowulf, the devils of Guthlac A are menacing forces which dwell in a "beorg" (Beowulf l. 2299b and Guthlac l. 148a, for example) [hill or barrow] which can be invaded by mankind, and Guthlac's actions, perceived from the devils' point of view, resemble those of Sigemund and Beowulf. The two Germanic heroes win the dragons' treasures, and Guthlac steals the "treasure" of the devils, that is, their last peaceful refuge in the wilderness. In Beowulf, Sigemund's invasion of the dragon's mound is a morally neutral event, although the poem's description of him as an "aglæca" suggests that it may be a wrong action, and the invasion of the dragon's mound by the "niðða nathwylc" (l. 2215a) [certain man] is clearly bad because it causes not only Beowulf's death but also the destruction of the Geatish nation. In contrast, Guthlac's invasion of the "beorg" and his theft of the devils' territory are presented as righteous actions, for Guthlac obeys the will of God.

Much critical discussion has centered on the imagery of the "beorg" in Guthlac A. Shook has interpreted the word as "barrow" and maintains that it stands "for all that is significant in the spiritual life of the good Christian: grace, struggle, the Will of God, temporal perseverance, and eternal salvation. His [the poet's] use of the barrow removes it from the category of a mere geographical appendage to a religious theme and makes it the center of the poem as poem."[37] In contrast, Paul F. Reichardt has argued that "the most appropriate rendering of the crucial term beorg may after all be the often-used 'mountain' because this reading creates important symbolic associations"[38] reminiscent of the ascetic vocabulary of John Cassian. Both Shook and Reichardt have concerned themselves exclusively with the Christian associations of the terminology of the poem, as has Karl P. Wentersdorf, who suggests that "the battle for the tumulus represents not merely the faithful Christian's spiritual war against his personal demons but also the unremitting campaign by the Church to suppress the lingering remnants of heathendom in England."[39] If my analysis be correct, however, the interpretation of "beorg" as "barrow" reminds us not only of the theological background of Guthlac A but also of the heroic vocabulary of Old English poetry. Because "beorg" is meaningful in both heroic and Christian contexts, its use in Guthlac A resonates with both implications, and we may appreciate the artistry of a poem which so deftly combines theology and heroic poetic language in its use of a single word. One who is interested in interpreting Guthlac A must be sensitive not only to the echoes of the Bible and of Patristic writings which have been analyzed by many scholars but also to the echoes of heroic poetry which, far from representing what Cherniss calls "only vestiges of heroic tradition" (p. 219), are part of the deep structures of the poem.

Another point at which the Christian and heroic traditions coincide in Guthlac A is in the description of the powerlessness of the forces of evil. In contrast to God, Who "an is ælmihtig" (l. 242a) [alone is Almighty], the devils are unable to do either good or evil. The theme of diabolic impotence recurs frequently in Christian literature; Sulpicius' Vita Martini, for example, describes all the malicious tricks the Devil used when "sanctum virum conabatur illudere" [he was striving to ridicule the holy man], but Martin was always able to recognize him "ut sive se in propria substantia contineret, sive in diversas figuras spiritualis nequitiæ transtulisset"[40] [whether he was contained in his own proper substance or whether he changed himself into various shapes of spiritual wickedness]. In Guthlac A, the Christian theme of diabolic impotence is expressed in language which recalls the theme of ineptitude found in heroic poetry. Beowulf is unable to use an ordinary sword to defeat his enemies but must rely on the fact that he has "þritiges / manna mægencræft on his mundgripe" (ll. 379b-80b) [the strength of thirty men in his hand-grip]. His very strength causes swords to break, except for the "sigeeadig bil, / eald sweord eotenisc" (ll. 1557b-58a) [the victory-famous blade, the old giant's sword] he uses against Grendel's dam. His inability to use the ordinary warrior's weapon shows that a hero is inept in ways in which an ordinary man is competent. Likewise, Grendel, despite his great strength, cannot "þone gifstol gretan" (l. 168) [approach the gift-stool] in Heorot.[41] Since Grendel is called a member of "Caines cynne" (l. 107a) [the race of Cain], the transference of heroic vocabulary to the depiction of Christian themes may already be operative in the depiction of his ineptitude. In Guthlac A, however, the transference is complete and the old heroic techniques are used to depict the Christian theme.

Although they are impotent and cannot "hine to deað deman" (1. 549) [judge him to death], the devils constantly threaten to slay Guthlac. Since they are unable to kill him, they carry him to "heldore" (1. 559b) [the door of Hell] and threaten "þæt he in þone grimman gryre gongan sceolde, / hweorfan gehyned to helwarum / 7 þær in bendum bryne þrowian" (11. 571a-73b) [that he should go into that grim horror, depart humbled to the dwellers in Hell and there endure burning in bonds]. Guthlac A's description of Hell resembles those in both Genesis B and Christ and Satan and must have reminded its original audience of common formulaic descriptions of Hell. Genesis B says that Hell is "sweartan" (1. 312b) [dark] and that the fiends suffer because of the "fyr edneowe" (1. 314b) [renewed fire]. Christ and Satan emphasizes that the damned endure "brynewelme" (1. 27a) [burning fire] and that they suffer "saran sorge" (1. 28a) [with great sorrow].

In Guthlac A, the devils are as powerless to damn Guthlac as they are to kill him, for salvation and damnation are in the power of God alone. Furthermore, only "æfter swyltcwale" (1. 561a) [after the agony of death] do the damned go to Hell, seeking an entrance "in þæt atule hus, / niþer under næssas neole grundas" (11. 562b-63b) [into that dreadful house, the deepest abysses down under the headlands]. A recurrent theme in Old English poetry describes Hell as a place "niþer under næssas." In Judith, for example, Holofernes' soul is sentenced to damnation:

    Læg se fula leap
gesne beæftan, gæst ellor hwearf
under neowelne næs ond ðær genyðerad wæs,
susle gesæled syððan æfre,

> wyrmum bewunden, witum gebunden,
> hearde gehæfted in hellebryne
> æfter hinsiðe.
> (ll. 111b-17a)

[The foul carcass lay empty behind, the spirit departed elsewhere under the deep headland and was brought low there, bound in torment ever afterwards, encircled with serpents, bound with torments, grievously chained in hell-fire after its journey hence].

In Beowulf, the theme describes not the Christian Hell but the terrifying other-world of Grendel's mere:

> Hie dygel lond
> warigeað wulfhleoþu, windige næssas,
> frecne fengelad, ðær fyrgenstream
> under næssa genipu niþer gewiteð,
> flod under foldan.
> (ll. 1357b-61a)

[They inhabit a secret land, wolf-slopes, windy headlands, dangerous fen-paths, where a mountain stream flows down under the darkness of the headlands, a river under the earth.]

The common theme presumably had an immediate impact on Guthlac A's audience, and its use in the poem represents another transfer of heroic vocabulary to theological use.

Guthlac is saved from the devils by God's intervention, for St. Bartholomew, "dryhtnes ar" (l. 684b) [the messenger of the Lord], is sent to proclaim "ufancunde ege earmum gæstum" (l. 686) [terror coming from above to the wretched spirits]. Furthermore, God rescues Guthlac specifically so that his soul may pass "in Godes wære" (l. 690b) [into the protection of God]. The end of Guthlac A describes a scene which balances that in which the devils threaten Guthlac with damnation although he has not yet died, for it describes Guthlac's apotheosis. Guthlac A never actually describes Guthlac's death but rather says that his soul is carried "engla fæðmum in uprodor" (l. 782) [in the arms of the angels into the firmament], with no mention of the fate of his body. The description of the journey of Guthlac's soul upwards is the exact opposite of Judith's description of the journey of Holofernes' soul downwards to Hell, and both must have been familiar to the Anglo-Saxon audience. Guthlac A's description of Guthlac's apotheosis also resembles religious works describing such incidents as the Assumption of Mary: "Assumpta est in celum anima beatae Mariae virginis cum psalmodiis, hymnis et canticis canticorum"[42] [The soul of the Blessed Virgin Mary was assumed into Heaven with psalms, hymns, and canticles of canticles]. The Assumption narratives were well known in Anglo-Saxon England, and it may be argued that they must have been familiar to the Guthlac A poet, for "various versions . . . [are] represented in English homilies,"[43] such as the thirteenth Blickling Homily, which describes how "Drihten bead þam wolcnum þæt hie eodan on neorxna wang & þær asetton þære eadigan Marian sawle"[44] [the Lord commanded the clouds to go to Paradise and place there the soul of the blessed Mary].

In addition to describing the constant warfare of angels and devils for the possession of Guthlac's soul and balancing its description of joy and sorrow and life and death, Guthlac A balances a pair of images against each other, those of the homeland and exile. In so doing, the poem introduces another heroic Germanic theme, that of Exile.[45] Guthlac A describes exile by using the verb "wrecan," "to drive" and, by extension, "to expel" or "to exile" and the noun "wræcc," an "exiled person," while it describes the homeland as "eðel" [homeland] or "eard" [home].[46] As Toby Christopher Langen has pointed out, Guthlac is a true saint who "perceives his life on earth as exile from God" (p. 44). As a result, he deliberately exiles

himself from other human beings--rejecting both
"man eall" (l. 96b) [all evil] and "eorðlic æþelu"
(l. 97a) [earthly nobility]--in order to devote
himself to God's service and win his true homeland.
While in his self-exile, he remains mindful of his
"ham in heofonum" (l. 98a) [dwelling in Heaven].
Guthlac establishes his hermitage in a place which
is not only that of his exile from men but also
that of the exile of the Fallen Angels, to whom
the poem refers as "wræcmæcgas" (l. 231b) [exiled
persons]. Exile is a persistent theme in Christian literature, for fallen man is exiled from
Paradise and the fallen angels from Heaven. The
Middle English <u>Robert of Sicily</u> suggests that
permanent exile from Heaven must be an unbearable
horror, for the angel who sits on King Robert's
throne during the latter's term of exile tells
Robert that "an hundred þousend" years of earthly
joy is not as great as the joy that is found in
Heaven "in an houre of a day."[47]

Throughout their disputes, Guthlac and the
devils explore the question of who is truly an
exile. The devils try to tempt him to despair by
emphasizing that it is he who lives in exile:

> Bi hwon scealt þu lifgan   þeah þu lond age?
> Ne þec mon hider   mose fedeð;
> beoð þe hungor 7 þurst   hearde gewinnan
> gif þu gewitest   swa wilde deor
> ana from eþele.
>   (ll. 273a-77a)

> [By what means will you live, although you
> possess this land? No one will feed you
> with food here; hunger and thirst will be
> a harsh opponent to you, if you depart like
> a wild beast alone from your homeland.]

Undisturbed by their threats, Guthlac points out
that it is the devils, not he, who are exiles and
that in the wasteland there are "wræcsetla fela, /
eardas onhæle   earmra gæsta" (ll. 296b-97b)
[many places of exile, secret homes of wretched

spirits]. When the devils take him to Hell, they tell him that he is such a sinful man that he does not deserve a "seld on swegle" (l. 585a) [seat in the sky]. In answer, he reminds them that they "wiðhogdum halgum dryhtne" (l. 631) [set themselves against the Holy Lord] and therefore "in wræcsiðe / longe lifdon" (ll. 623b-24a) [have lived for a long time on the journey of exile].

The devils, who were punished "fore oferhygdum" (l. 634a) [because of their pride], remind us not only of the fallen angels of Christian tradition but also of the human villains of Old English poetry. Holofernes in Judith, for example, is "swiðmod" (l. 30a) [harsh of mind], behaves like a beast during his lifetime, and is sentenced to Hell after his death. Furthermore, the devils are "dreame bidrorene" (l. 626a) [deprived of joy] and are the enemies of everything good, and they resemble the monsters of the heroic tradition. They most closely resemble Grendel, who is "dreamum bedæled" (l. 721a) [deprived of joys], and Beowulf's dragon, which is called "se ðeodsceaða" (l. 2278a) [the enemy of the people]. Although Beowulf shows considerable Christian influence and Grendel is, indeed, one of "Caines cynne" (l. 107a) [the kin of Cain], James David Mason has studied at length "the nature of the monstrous"[48] in the poem and shown that it is also influenced by pre-Christian traditions.

Mason compares the Old English depiction of monsters to those found in Old Norse works, pointing out that even though "Old Norse, like Old English, came to be written down only in Christian times . . . [we have] evidence paralleling that of written literature but dating from pagan times: stone carvings and metal-work . . . [which indicate] that monster-combats have an origin in pre-Christian times" (p. 53). According to Mason, the typical Old Norse monster is an exile, an anthropomorphic shape-shifter, and a being who taunts the hero before they fight; in fact, the taunt can be a "replacement for the monster-combat" (p. 17).

Mason points out that in the semi-historical sagas, "the role of monster sometimes falls to an otherwise relatively normal man, if he chances to be outlawed. As outlaw, he becomes a vargr, and vargr . . . means both 'wolf' and 'outlaw' in Old Norse. The outlawed man may not himself be a berserkr; he may not even show any tendencies to shape-shifting. But he nonetheless fills the monster's role" (pp. 170-71).

Mason discusses the fact that "Grendel is twice an exile: in his own separation from men and in his unpleasant company, that déofla gedræg [company of devils] among whom he suffers and dies" (p. 131). Grendel's exile has Christian implications, because Grendel lives among the devils, who are exiled from God; Mason comments that "Grendel is called wergan gást [accursed spirit] . . . once early in the poem when the hearer should still have Cain's name echoing in his ears" (p. 145). In Genesis B, in which, as Mason points out, "Cain's kin are called wergum folk" (p. 131), "werga" also has Christian connotations. Nevertheless, it has connotations not associated with Christianity, for it is "cognate with Old Norse vargr . . . [which] means principally '(were)wolf' . . . 'Transgressor' is a derivative meaning. The outlaw, by his crime, makes a werewolf of himself, as his crime makes him something less than human" (p. 145). Thus, Grendel's exile is similar to that of Old Norse outlaws.

As has been discussed, Guthlac's devils live "in wræcsiðe" (l. 623b) [on the journey of exile] just as do Grendel and the Old Norse "vargar." Like Grendel, they are described by the word which means "wolf," "outlaw," and "accursed being"; Guthlac addresses them as "awyrgde" (l. 255a) [outlawed or accursed ones], and the poet refers to one of them as "se werga gæst" (l. 451a) [the outlawed or accursed spirit]. With this word, therefore, the poet depicts the devils as both outlawed from a heroic point of view and damned from a Christian one. The devils are beings whom Mason describes in the title of his study as "Monsters with Human Voices" who taunt and abuse the hero; at one point, for example, the devils "ligesearwum / ahofun hearmstafas" (ll. 228b-29a) [with cunning lies raised up afflictions]. Like Old Norse monsters, the devils are generally anthropomorphic but have bestial characteristics, as when they threaten that diabolic hosts will destroy Guthlac:

>   We þas wic magun
> fotum afyllan: folc inðriceð
> meara þreatum   7 monfarum.
> Beoð þa gebolgne   þa þec breodwiað,
> tredað þec 7 tergað   7 hyra torn wrecað,
> toberað þec blodgum lastum.
>   (ll. 284b-89a)

[We can level the dwelling with our feet: the people will force a way in with troops of horses and moving hosts. Then those who strike you down will be enraged, they will trample and torment you and wreak their anger, and they will bear you off leaving bloody tracks.]

Mason points out that the Old Norse Vǫluspá describes those "who deserve outlawry" (p. 63), including "menn meinsvara" [oathbreakers]; the devils of Guthlac A are twice called "wærlogan" (ll. 298a and 623a) [oathbreakers].

A final point that links the Christian story of Guthlac's combat against the devils with pre-Christian stories of monster combats is that in the latter the hero is, in Mason's words, not "so essentially different from the monster that he could not become like his adversary" (p. 38); in Mesopotamian and Norse literature, "both attacking enemy or monster and defending god or hero may have beast-characteristics" (p. 71). When the devils try to convince Guthlac that he, rather than they, is the true exile, they are trying to convince him

that he is a monster; they compare him to a "wilde
deor" (l. 276b) [wild beast], implying that he has
"beast-characteristics." Likewise, they tempt him
to join the "wræcmæcgas" (l. 129b) [exiled persons],
suggesting to him "þæt he sceaðena gemot / nihtes
sohte 7 þurh neþinge / wunne æfter worulde"
(ll. 127b-29a) [that he should seek the assembly
of criminals at night and by boldness strive for
the world]. As all Christians know, no human being
is so different from the devils that he cannot
become like them by sinning, so that Guthlac is in
danger of becoming an "aglæca" or a "vargr" like
each of those who tempt him.

    After the devils make their final attempt to
terrify Guthlac and exile him from God's protection, God shows clearly that Guthlac is not exiled
from it, for He sends St. Bartholomew to order the
devils to return Guthlac to his hermitage, which
is now a "sigewong" (l. 742a) [victorious plain]
that resembles the Paradise which men lost when
they became exiled from God. The imagery of exile
in Guthlac A is one of the image clusters in which
Christian and heroic ideas reverberate simultaneous-
ly. As Cherniss points out, "the heroic concept
of exile as a state of utmost deprivation and misery
appears to function as a metaphor for their [the
devils'] spiritual situation" (p. 232), but the
imagery of exile has a Christian background as well
in both the Book of Job and the New Testament
account of Christ's wanderings in the wilderness.
The Guthlac A poet has, therefore, expressed a
concept familiar to him from both Biblical narratives and heroic poetry. After the Fall, man was
exiled from Paradise, and his only way to return
there is to exile himself from normal, but sinful,
human life. Guthlac's hermitage, which is far
from his earthly home and "bimiþen fore monnum"
(l. 147a) [concealed from men], is described as
Paradise and a "haligne ham" (l. 149) [holy
dwelling]. John Bugge suggests that Guthlac A,
like The Phoenix, expresses the theme "of Paradise
as the natural homeland of the monk . . . [which]
is one of the two guiding principles of contempo-

rary monastic spirituality (the other being life as exile or peregrinatio)";[49] thus, the imagery of exile and Paradise, expressed in formulaic terms, helps establish both the monastic concerns of Guthlac A and the fact that the poem is intended for a properly-trained audience capable of appreciating both strands of imagery.

The beginning of The Phoenix describes Paradise--called "neorxnawong"[50] (l. 397a) [the paradisaical plain] at the end of the poem--as a region which is not "mongum gefere / folcagendra" (ll. 4b-5a) [accessible to many earth-dwellers]. Like Guthlac's hermitage, the Phoenix's Paradise is under the rule of "Meotud" (l. 6a) [the Measurer] and "afyrred is / þurh Meotudes meaht manfremmendum" (ll. 5b-6b) [is removed from evildoers by the power of the Measurer]. After Guthlac wins his victory, his hermitage is described with the formulaic half-line, "smolt wæs se sigewong" (l. 742a) [peaceful was the field of victory], a phrase which is appropriate in the Christian-heroic context of Guthlac A. The same formulaic half-line, however, appears in The Phoenix, which says "smylte is se sigewong" (l. 33a) [peaceful is the field of victory] after its description of Paradise, and The Phoenix's use of the term seems at first inappropriate because the poem describes neither a battlefield nor a "sigewong." Latin works describe the hermitages of the great ascetic saints in terms of Paradise, and Old English poetry uses its traditional heroic vocabulary to describe their lives. It seems, therefore, natural to find the heroic terms used in Guthlac A also used in the less appropriate context of The Phoenix. In addition, The Phoenix's use of the present-tense "is" emphasizes the fact that the earthly Paradise remains a "sigewong" at all times, whereas Guthlac A's use of the past-tense "wæs" emphasizes the fact that at that moment his hermitage became a paradisaical "sigewong."

The devils are permanently exiled both from the eternal joys of Heaven and from any pleasant worldly dwelling place, for Guthlac's "sigewong" is the place of their defeat. Guthlac can "eardes brucan" (1. 745b) [enjoy his home] because he and it are "in Godes wære" (1. 746b) [in the protection of God], and after his death he wins the eternal homeland the devils have forfeited and a "setl on swegle" (1. 785a) [seat in Heaven]. Although Guthlac and the devils inhabit the wasteland at the same time, they are on journeys in opposite directions: the devils are moving away from Heaven at the same time as Guthlac is moving towards it, and the former are on a journey which ends in eternal exile while the latter is on one which ends in the <u>comitatus</u> of Heaven.

<u>Guthlac A</u> uses much imagery concerned with payment and repayment, which it introduces in the prologue with the statement about "lænan dreamas" (1. 3a) [transitory joys; that is, joys which have been lent]. The prologue describes the soul to whom an "ece lean" (1. 15b) [eternal reward] has been given, and the end of the poem echoes this idea when Guthlac earns Heaven as his "lean" (1. 784b) [reward]. In the middle portion of the poem, the devils threaten Guthlac with "deaþa gedal" (1. 235a) [the allotment of death] and say that they will "Guðlace forgiefan" (1. 327) [repay Guthlac] for stealing their refuge. However, the poem makes it clear that it is the devils themselves who are deprived not only of heavenly joys but also of "lænan dreamas," for their last refuge on earth is consecrated to God's service by Guthlac. Likewise, although they say that they will give him "womma gehwylces / lean" (ll. 587b-88a) [repayment for every sinful act], God has already repaid them for their sinful acts by depriving them of Heaven. The poem thus emphasizes the ironic fact that the devils impotently threaten to do to Guthlac what God has done to them already; it describes the ironic inversion of the hopes of the devils and thereby emphasizes the sanctity of Guthlac.

In contrast to the framework of <u>Guthlac A</u>, which makes general statements about <u>righteous</u>

people and the joys of Heaven that they may expect, the middle portion focuses on the specific example of Guthlac by describing how he lives and wins victories against the devils. <u>Guthlac A</u> develops, to quote Tolkien's description of <u>Beowulf</u>, as "a simple and <u>static</u> structure" (p. 81) that presents balanced pictures of such ideas as joy and suffering, exile and the homeland, and angelic guardians and demonic persecutors. <u>Guthlac A</u> presents the practice of ascetic virtues as the most desirable life and is, therefore, homiletic. At the same time, its homiletic remarks develop the themes of the narrative portions of the poem and contribute to the affective qualities thereof. <u>Guthlac A</u> describes a secular hero who left the world to become one of the heroes of the Church, applies the language of heroic poetry to his ascetic life, and finally shows that it is better to be a saint than a warrior because a saint can earn life after death. One fully heroic poem, <u>La Chanson de Roland</u>, makes a similar point, for it describes a hero who learns that his heroism is inadequate, and who finally repents and dies a saintly death.[51] In contrast to the <u>Roland</u>, however, <u>Guthlac A</u> depicts a man who rejects earthly heroism at an early age and refuses to fight against the devils with the weapons of a warrior:

> No ic eow sweord ongean
> mid gebolgne hond oðberan þence,
> worulde wæpen, ne sceal þes wong Gode
> þurh blodgyte gebuen weorðan
> ac ic minum Criste cweman þence
> leofran lace.
> (ll. 302b-7a)

> [I do not intend to bear a sword, a worldly weapon, against you with an angry hand, nor will this plain be occupied for God by means of bloodshed, but I intend to please my Christ with a better offering.]

Since "lac" is often used to describe swordplay, Guthlac is thus playing with the meanings of the term: he has rejected the warrior's "lac" for that of Christian sacrifice. The poem is carefully structured to answer the question posed at its beginning: how can a man who "his gæste forð / weges willian" (ll. 36b-37a) [has desires about the forthcoming journey of his soul] be saved? The answer finally is that, although there are many "hadas under heofonum" (l. 31a) [ranks under Heaven], only that of a holy hermit can assure salvation. The Christian and heroic language and images work together to make the audience wish to obey the call to live an eremitical life.

Section C
The Eternal Return:
The Mythic Background

From the point of view outlined above, Guthlac A is an effective literary work which uses the heroic Germanic vocabulary to express concerns drawn from the Graeco-Roman Christian world. In addition, however, it has a mythic dimension, because Guthlac, like other epic heroes of the Indo-European world, has been mythicized, and he accordingly re-enacts exploits of the archetypal hero and god.

Guthlac is presumably a historical figure, although most of the information about him is found in Felix's Vita Sancti Guthlaci.[52] Like many other saints in famous hagiographic works, Felix's Guthlac is mythicized: his birth is marked by a golden-red hand which comes from Heaven and blesses the door of the house where his mother lies in labor, he has the ability to perform miracles, and he fights repeatedly against monsters in the form of the devils who assail him in the wasteland. According to Mircea Eliade, the

mythicization of historical figures is a common
process, so that "the historical character of the
persons celebrated in epic poetry is not in question. But their historicity does not long resist
the corrosive action of mythicization. . . . The
historical personage is assimilated to his mythical model . . . while the event is identified
with the category of mythical actions (fight with
monster, enemy brothers, etc.)."[53] Eliade further
points out that when "we witness the metamorphosis
of a historical figure into a mythical hero,"
certain events occur, for "supernatural elements
[are] summoned to reinforce . . . [the] legends"
(p. 42). One "familiar paradigmatic myth recounts
the combat between the hero and a gigantic serpent,
often three-headed, sometimes replaced by a marine
monster" (p. 37), which represents chaos. In
other stories, the chaos-monsters are depicted as
other beasts; for example, the Egyptians called
the Pharaoh's enemies "'sons of ruin, wolves, dogs,'
and so forth" (p. 37). Like authors of works about
Near Eastern heroes, Felix depicts Guthlac's
battles against the devils as a hero's fight
against the chaos-monster.

It seems likely that the Guthlac A poet knew
Felix's Vita,[54] and he therefore knew the mythicized version of the saint whom he celebrated in
his heroic poem. His description of Guthlac's
fight against the devils for possession of the
wasteland focuses on it in greater detail than the
Vita does, for in the latter it is only one of a
series of events from the saint's life. The devils
against whom Guthlac fights are beast-like and
represent chaos, for they are "reowe to ræsanne /
gifrum grapum" (ll. 406a-7a) [fierce to attack with
greedy grasps]. Their noises--"breahtm" (l. 262a)
[tumult], "woð" (l. 263b) [sound], and "cirm"
(l. 264a) [clamor]--contain no words and are therefore beastlike and chaotic. Guthlac must fight
against the devils because he has established a
hermitage in the "dygle stow" (l. 215a) [secret
spot] where they have a refuge. After he does so,
the devils are no longer able "on eorþan eardes

brucan" (l. 220) [to enjoy a home on earth]. Guthlac is establishing a new creation, and he is called "se bytla . . . / se þær haligne ham arærde" (ll. 148b-49b) [the builder who raised up the holy dwelling there]. The devils are clearly, in Eliade's words, to be "identified with the 'masters of the ground,' with the autochthons against whom the newcomers, the 'conquerors,' those who are to form (i.e., create) the occupied territories, must fight" (p. 40). Likewise, Guthlac is the newcomer who conquers the autochthons, resembling Beowulf, who fights against Grendel and his dam on behalf of the Danes after the latter occupied the territory of the monsters by building Heorot. The Christian story of the fight of a saint against the devils, described formulaically as the fight of a Germanic hero against monsters, derives extra impact from the fact that it depicts a re-enactment of the primordial struggle of the hero-creator against the beings who represent chaos.

Because Guthlac is depicted as a mythicized hero, we might expect <u>Guthlac A</u> to be organized around a mythic pattern; indeed, the structure and imagery of the poem are governed by what Eliade calls "the myth of the eternal return" (p. 141). As Michael N. Nagler points out in his study of Homer, this "common myth of the hero who departs, is vitally missed by his people while himself undergoing sore trials, and returns in triumph provides the main movement of many, perhaps, in a sense, of all heroic myths."[55] The myth lies deep in the structures of <u>Guthlac A</u>, and the second element--that the hero "is vitally missed by his people"--is almost non-existent. However, in Nagler's words, "the traditional pattern is not an inert skeleton made into a poetic performance by the mere filling in of appropriate details. . . . A traditional plot pattern itself is more a Gestalt than a rigid formula" (p. 132). The use of the pattern in <u>Guthlac A</u> is most easily understood when compared to the use thereof in other works familiar to all students of epic, like the <u>Odyssey</u>.

Guthlac is a hero and champion who fights against the enemies of his land; his hermitage is described as his "eorðlic eþel" (l. 261a) [homeland on earth], and he is "Cristes cempa" (l. 153a) [Christ's champion] who conquers and then holds a land. As such, he is analogous to Odysseus, king of Ithaka and leader of his people. Like Odysseus, Guthlac departs from his land under compulsion; both belong to the group that Vladimir Propp calls "victimized heroes."[56] Just as Odysseus in his wanderings visits the other-world when he voyages from Lotus-land to Phaiakia and even to Hades itself, Guthlac visits the other-world, for the devils take him to the door of Hell. Likewise, as Kalypso wishes to keep Odysseus on Ogygia, the devils wish to force Guthlac to remain in Hell. During this journey, Guthlac undergoes what Nagler calls "sore trials," and the devils threaten to make him suffer "in ðam grimmestan gæstgewinne" (l. 589) [in the cruellest soul-torment].

The Olympian gods release Odysseus from his imprisonment by sending the divine messenger Hermes to order Kalypso to free him. Similarly, God sends St. Bartholomew, "dryhtnes ar" (l. 684b) [the messenger of the Lord], to order the devils "eft hraðe unscyldigne / of þam wræcsiðe wuldres cempan / lædan limhalne" (ll. 687a-89a) [to bring back quickly the guiltless champion of glory from the journey of exile with whole limbs]. Like Odysseus, Guthlac returns to the home for which he longs, "to þam onwillan eorðan dæle" (l. 728) [to the wished-for portion of the earth], and restores order there. The world in which Guthlac sets things right after his return is that of the birds, not of men, in what Stanley B. Greenfield calls a "pacific scene of home welcoming by the forest denizens":[57]

       Sigehreðig cwom
  bytla to þam beorge; hine bletsadon
  monge mægwlitas meaglum reordum,
  treofugla tuddor tacnum cyðdon

> eadges eftcyme;   oft he him æte heold
> þonne hy him hungrige   ymb hond flugon,
> gradum gifre   geoce gefegon.
> (ll. 732b-38b)

[Rejoicing in victory, the builder came to
the barrow; many species blessed him with
earnest voices, the races of forest birds
made known by signs the return of the
blessed one; often he held food for them
when they, hungry, flew around his hands;
greedily eager, they rejoiced in his aid.]

As Woolf has pointed out, this passage represents a "return to a paradisal relationship between man and the animals" (p. 57), but many critics find it disturbing because it is not a typical piece of Old English poetry, resembling only the description of the earthly paradise in The Phoenix.[58] Woolf suggests that "the passage is too short and too abruptly introduced for it to carry full weight or to be in proportion to the rest" (p. 57). If, however, we view the passage as the description of the return of the hero, we realize that it is neither abruptly introduced nor too short; as the audience of a poem composed in the heroic, epic style, we know that the hero must return and restore order to his land, and we have been expecting him to do so ever since he departed in the custody of the devils. Since the story of the return of the hero has no rigid pattern, the elements do not have to be of any particular length in order to be "in proper proportion" to each other.

Because the focus of Guthlac A is always on Guthlac, we do not see the way in which his presence is "vitally missed" by the denizens of his land; similarly, we would not know the conditions in Ithaka if the Odyssey began with Book V instead of with the Telemachy. However, we can deduce the lack which is caused by Guthlac's departure, for the birds would have had no one to feed them during his absence. Because it underplays the element of lack, Guthlac A is almost closer to the archetypal pattern which lies behind the myth of the hero who returns than to the myth itself; Lord has described it as "the story pattern of the god who dies, wanders for a period of time in the other world, and then returns" (p. 186). Guthlac does not die, but he does visit a place where men usually go only after death, stays there for a "period of time," and then returns to the world.

Unlike the Odyssey, Guthlac A does not end with the return of the hero and the re-establishment of order in the homeland. Instead, it describes Guthlac's journey to his true homeland "in uprodor" (l. 782b) [in Heaven above]. Within a Christian framework, it is not enough for the hero to re-enact the secular pattern of return as a hero like Odysseus does. Instead, he must re-enact the archetypal pattern established by Christ, the God Who was born into human life and wandered in the world, died on Good Friday, was resurrected and wandered on earth for forty more days, and finally returned to His heavenly home, which Guthlac A describes as "lifgendra lond" (l. 818) [the land of the living] in contrast to this world of death. Guthlac accordingly follows Christ and receives a "setl on swegle" (l. 785a) [seat in Heaven]. Since all men were exiled from Paradise after the Fall and are wandering in the "other world" of this earth, all should be trying to return to Paradise with a fervor analogous to that with which Odysseus tried to return to Ithaka. The poem ends with a general admonition to follow in Christ's footsteps and earn the right to return to the true homeland and share its ordered existence:

>   Swa soðfæstra   sawla motun
>   in ecne geard, up gestigan,
>   rodera rice,   þa þe ræfnað her
>   wordum 7 weorcum   wuldorcyninges
>   lare longsume   on hyra lifes tid,
>   earniað on eorðan   ecan lifes,
>   hames in heahþu.
>   (ll. 790a-96a)

[Thus the souls of the righteous may rise
up into the eternal dwelling-place, the
kingdom of the heavens, those who perform
here during the time of their life in words
and works the enduring teaching of the King
of glory, earn while on earth eternal life,
a dwelling on high.]

Section D
Guthlac A:
The Composite View

When we consider the backgrounds of Guthlac
A--the direct ones from monastic and heroic writings and the more indirect mythic one--we realize
that Guthlac A is truly a heroic poem and that
Guthlac is a hero in terms of all three traditions.
Guthlac A is carefully shaped to show that the
monastic vocation is the only "had" in which it is
possible for men to be heroes and win salvation
because they "Cristes æ / lærað 7 læstað 7 his
lof rærað" (ll. 23b-24b) [teach and follow the law
of Christ and raise up His praise], and it has been
influenced by the most important of early monastic
texts: St. Benedict's Regula Monachorum. Guthlac
A is not concerned with the everyday details of
monastic life, and, because it describes none of
the details of Guthlac's eremitical routine, it
contains no passages which correspond to those
which in the Regula describe the governance of a
monastery. Instead, it follows those passages
which present the purpose and psychological under-
pinnings of monasticism. For example, the very
beginning of the Regula is an invitation to the
reader to become a soldier of Christ: "Ad te ergo
nunc meus sermo dirigitur, quisquis abrenuntians
propriis voluntatibus, Domino Christo vero regi
militaturus, obedientiæ fortissima atque præclara

arma assumis"⁵⁹ [My word is therefore directed to
you, whoever you may be, so that, giving up your
own will you take up the bright and very strong
weapons of obedience and fight for the true King,
our Lord Christ]. Guthlac rejects the sword, the
"worulde wæpen" (l. 304a) [worldly weapon], and
girds himself with "gæstlicum / wæpnum" (ll. 177b-
78a) [spiritual weapons] to fight against the
devils. Although Guthlac A makes it clear that
Guthlac is not a worldly warrior, it nevertheless
calls him a "cempa" (l. 180b) [champion] when it
describes how he uses his "fortissima atque
præclara arma" to overcome "frecnessa fela"
(l. 181a) [many perils]. Guthlac A makes appropriate use of the formulas and themes of Old
English heroic poetry to describe Guthlac's eremitical life, and in the passages influenced by the
Regula Monachorum, it uses the heroic vocabulary
to express the idea of Christian heroism. In
addition, Guthlac repeats the archetypal pattern
of the return of the hero, a fact which links him
to the heroes of Indo-European myths. Many saints
re-enact the life of Christ in their own lives; in
Albertson's words, "behind the hero is always a
god" (p. 25). Just as behind a pagan hero like
Odysseus is a pagan god, behind a Christian hero-
saint is Christ.

Many interpretations of Guthlac A fall short
of complete credibility because they isolate only
one strand of influence on the poem. Reichardt,
for example, has maintained that Guthlac A expresses ideas about eremiticism which correspond
to "the aims of the eremetic life as defined in the
conferences of John Cassian" (p. 332), Thundyil and
Post have argued convincingly that the poem is influenced by the Regula Monachorum, Shook has
suggested that the angelology is indebted to "the
tradition represented by the Visio Sancti Pauli,"⁶⁰
and Langen is interested in analyzing "the patristic resonance" (p. 27) of both Guthlac A and B. I
submit, however, that perceiving the way in which
the poet uses the monastic, heroic, and mythic
elements of his literary traditions to express his
didactic message helps us to appreciate what Calder

has described as "the true metamorphosis that occurred when Anglo-Saxon scops wrought poetry from Latin prose models."[61] Guthlac A is an effective and moving argument in favor of the monastic life and a poem of unusual power and beauty.

Guthlac A is effective because it not only fulfills the expectations of its audience and expresses its didactic message but also goes beyond the expectations and manipulates the sympathies of the audience. Like Beowulf, it makes us sympathize with the enemies of mankind, in this case, with the devils who have been dispossessed of their homeland, even though we know that Guthlac performs God's will when he sends them into exile. Furthermore, it not only uses themes aesthetically, but also organizes the structure and imagery of the poem around the formulaic theme of Exile, which is one of the points at which the Christian subject matter and the traditional poetic language converge: Guthlac is in self-exile as a hermit and the devils are permanently exiled from God's favor. Guthlac A uses the theme of the Cliff of Death in a way that captures what Adrien Bonjour has called "the full force of . . . [the] associational powers"[62] of a theme, recalling both the terrifying other-world of Grendel's mere and the Christian Hell to which Holofernes' soul is sentenced. Since the members of the original Old English audience of Guthlac A must have been familiar with many more instances of the Cliff of Death than is a modern reader, the theme must have evoked an even greater sense of horror and doom for them than it does for us. In addition, Guthlac A plays with multiple meanings of its terminology in a way which enhances its didactic purpose, and it may, of course, use word-play which we are no longer able to recognize and appreciate. It uses the poetic devices available to the Old English poet to show that only a Christian monk can conquer the Cliff of Death and escape from the pattern of exile which has trapped all post-lapsarian men, including the heroic warrior. The poem ends with a description of the joys that the blessed experience "on lifgendra londes wynne" (l. 818) [in the joy of the land of the living], and because it ends in Heaven and does not return to the misery of the world, Guthlac A is a positive presentation of the Christian message. It is, in fact, in the same tradition as the greatest of all Christian poems, The Divine Comedy, which ends with a vision of the ineffable splendor of Heaven and "l'amor che move il sole e l'altre stelle"[63] [the Love which moves the sun and the other stars].

Notes to Chapter Two

¹Theodor Wolpers, *Die Englische Heiligenlegende des Mittelalters* (Tübingen: Max Niemeyer, 1964), p. 115. All further references appear in the text.

²Lawrence K. Shook, "The Prologue of the Old-English 'Guthlac A'," *MS*, 23 (1961), pp. 296 and 295.

³Frances Randall Lipp, "Guthlac A: An Interpretation," *MS*, 33 (1971), p. 62. All further references appear in the text.

⁴Bede, *Vita Sancti Cuthberti*, *Two Lives of Saint Cuthbert: A Life by an Anonymous Monk of Lindisfarne and Bede's Prose Life*, ed. Bertram Colgrave (New York: Greenwood Press, 1969), pp. 164-65. All further references appear in the text; the translations used are those of Colgrave.

⁵In "Bede and the Vernacular," *Famulus Christi: Essays in Commemoration of the Thirteenth Centenary of the Birth of the Venerable Bede*, ed. Gerald Bonner (London: SPCK, 1976), André Crépin reminds his reader that "Bede is said to have died while dictating English translations" (p. 170). He theorizes that "Bede's attitude to the vernacular prompted the writing-down of Old English Christian poetry and it permitted . . . the flowering of Old English translations encouraged by King Alfred" (p. 186).

⁶George Herzfeld, ed. and trans., *An Old English Martyrology*, EETS, Old Series vol. 116 (London: The Early English Text Society, 1900; rpt. Millwood, New York: Kraus Reprint Co., 1975), p. x.

⁷Fred C. Robinson, "Some Uses of Name-Meanings in Old English Poetry," *NM*, 69 (1968), p. 168.

⁸All quotations from the Bible are from Biblia Sacra, Vulgatae Editionis (Rome: Editiones Paulinae, 1957); all translations are mine.

⁹Cynthia Edelstein Cornell, "Sources of the Old English Guthlac Poems" (Diss. Univ. of Missouri-Columbia, 1976), p. 189. All further references appear in the text.

¹⁰Zacharias P. Thundyil, C. M. I., Covenant in Anglo-Saxon Thought (Madras, Bombay, Calcutta, and Delhi: The Macmillan Co. of India, Ltd., 1972), p. 178. I find myself in agreement with the view of Thundyil, rather than with that of Roberts, who states that "Felix's life of Guthlac places the saint in the Antonian rather than the Benedictine monastic tradition" and that Guthlac A and B are both "glorifying the same tradition" [The Guthlac Poems, p. 10].

¹¹Thomas R. Post, "The Benedictine Influence on Guthlac A," unpublished paper, quoted with Post's permission, pp. 1-2.

¹²Krapp and Dobbie, The Exeter Book, p. xxx.

¹³Krapp and Dobbie, The Exeter Book, p. xxx.

¹⁴R. K. Gordon, trans., Anglo-Saxon Poetry (London: J. M. Dent and Sons, Ltd., 1970), pp. 163-64 and 256. Gordon follows the arrangement of the edition of Christian W. M. Grein, Bibliothek der Angelsächischen Poesie (Leipzig: Georg H. Wigand, 1897), vol. 3, pp. 53-55.

¹⁵See especially Shook, "Prologue," pp. 1-10; Cornell, "Sources," pp. 67-69; and Toby Christopher Langen, "A Commentary on the Two Old English Poems on St. Guðlac" (Diss. Univ. of Washington, 1973), pp. 28-30. All references to Langen's "Commentary" appear in the text.

¹⁶Guthlac begins with a large initial capital letter, and most of its first line is capitalized. As a result, there is a definite division between

it and the end of Christ III, but there is no such division between lines 29 and 30. As Krapp and Dobbie say, "there can be little doubt that he [the compiler] intended this passage . . . to be part of the major division of the manuscript which begins at this point and continues with the life of Guthlac" (The Exeter Book, p. xxx).

[17] Calder, "Guthlac A and Guthlac B," p. 67.

[18] F. R. Hoare, trans., The Western Fathers, The Makers of Christendom, ed. Christopher Dawson (New York: Sheed and Ward, 1954), p. 3.

[19] Edmund Spenser, The Faerie Queene, Book VII, Canto viii, l. 6, in Poetical Works, ed. J. C. Smith and E. De Selincourt (London: Oxford Univ. Press, 1966), p. 406.

[20] "Had" is a difficult word to translate. According to Ferdinand Holthausen, Altenglisches Etymologisches Wörterbuch, 2nd. ed. (Heidelberg: Carl Winter, 1963), p. 143, it can mean "person; rang, stand, würde, amt; zustand, natur, form, art; geschlecht, familie, stamm; chor." The most common meanings used in Guthlac A are "person" and "rank" and the extended meaning, "monastic vocation."

[21] Calder, "Guthlac A and Guthlac B," p. 67.

[22] R. W. Chambers, Max Förster, and Robin Flower, eds., The Exeter Book of Old English Poetry (London: Percy, Lund, Humphries, and Co., 1933), p. 65.

[23] George K. Anderson, The Literature of the Anglo-Saxons (Princeton, New Jersey: Princeton Univ. Press, 1949), p. 136. All further references appear in the text.

[24] Shook, "Prologue," p. 295.

[25] Calder, "Guthlac A and Guthlac B," p. 77.

[26] The question of the means whereby Beowulf was composed has been debated ever since Magoun pub-

lished "Oral-Formulaic Character of Anglo-Saxon Narrative Poetry" in 1953. The best statement of the prevailing modern view has been made by Renoir in "Beowulf: A Contextual Introduction to Its Contents and Techniques" (Oinas, ed., Heroic Epic and Saga, p. 107), in which he says, "the mechanics and contents of the poem conform to the principles of oral-formulaic composition, but it must be repeated that the experts are by no means in agreement about the actual mode of composition of the text as we know it."

[27] J. R. R. Tolkien, "Beowulf: The Monsters and the Critics," Proceedings of the British Academy, 22 (1936), rpt. in Lewis E. Nicholson, ed., An Anthology of Beowulf Criticism (Notre Dame: Univ. of Notre Dame Press, 1963), p. 81. All further references appear in the text.

[28] Joan Blomfield, "The Style and Structure of Beowulf," Review of English Studies, 14 (1938), rpt. in Donald K. Fry, The Beowulf Poet: A Collection of Critical Essays (Englewood Cliffs, N.J.: Prentice-Hall, Inc., 1968), p. 57.

[29] Renoir, "Beowulf: A Contextual Introduction," p. 104.

[30] In "Some Notes and Queries on the Uses of Irony," In Geardagum II: Essays on Old and Middle English Language and Literature, ed. Loren C. Gruber and Dean Loganbill (Denver: The Society for New Language Study, 1978), Robert P. Black maintains that throughout Guthlac A "the conflict is essentially psychological" (p. 54) and is influenced by Prudentius' Psychomachia. In contrast, I am suggesting that the conflict is not psychological, but as real as those between Beowulf and Grendel or Gilgamesh and Humbaba.

[31] Calder, "Guthlac A and Guthlac B," p. 69.

[32] See Langen, "Commentary," pp. 29ff.

³³The Pœnitentiale Ecgberti Archepiscopi Eboracensis glosses the phrase "ordinatus homo" with "ȝehaðoð man" and the phrase "et ordinem susceperit" with "to hade fenȝ" [Ancient Laws and Institutes of England, vol. 2, ed. Benjamin Thorpe (England: The Commissioners on the Public Records of the Kingdom, 1840), pp. 206-7].

³⁴Wulfstan, Sermo Lupi Ad Anglos, ed. Dorothy Whitelock (London: Methuen and Co., Ltd., 1939), p. 61. The meaning vocation becomes common during the Middle English period, for Orm speaks of "kannunkes had and lif" [the vocation and life of a canon] [The Ormulum, with the Notes and Glossary of Dr. R. M. White, ed. Robert Holt (Oxford: At the Clarendon Press, 1878), vol. 1, p. B]. The author of Cursor Mundi says that St. Mark was "o biscop siþen he tok þe hade" [a bishop after he took orders] [Cursor Mundi, Four Versions, ed. Richard Morris, EETS, Old Series vol. 66 (Oxford: The Early English Text Society, 1874, rpt. 1961), p. 1216].

³⁵According to Joseph Bosworth, ed., An Anglo-Saxon Dictionary, enlarged by T. Northcote Toller with revised and enlarged addenda by Alister Campbell (Oxford: The Univ. Press, 1973), p. 29, ag translates the Latin nequitia, so that aglac is "worthless play" and, by extension, misery, trouble, or vexation. An aglaca is, therefore, a being characterized by misery or torment.

³⁶Marion Lois Huffines, "OE āglǣce: Magic and Moral Decline of Monsters and Men," Semasia, 1 (1974), p. 80.

³⁷Shook, "The Burial Mound in Guthlac A," MP, 58 (1960), p. 10.

³⁸Paul F. Reichardt, "Guthlac A and the Landscape of Spiritual Perfection," Neophilologus, 58 (1974), p. 331. All further references appear in the text.

[39] Karl P. Wentersdorf, "Guthlac A: The Battle for the Beorg," Neophilologus, 62 (1978), p. 136.

[40] Sulpicius Severus, De Vita Beati Martini, Liber Unus, Patrologiae Cursus Completus, vol. 20, ed. J.-P. Migne (Paris: Venit Apud Editorem, 1845), col. 172.

[41] In his edition of Beowulf, Charles L. Wrenn moves lines 168a-69b from their location in the manuscript to expand "the remarks about Cain which end at l. 110 . . . [because] the inserted lines fit Cain, but not Grendel or Hrothgar in the context of ll. 166-70. . . . [After l. 110] clearly is their right place--whether they are a genuine remark of the poet, or the explanation or gloss of an interpreter" [Beowulf With the Finnesburg Fragment, 2nd. ed. (London: George C. Harrap and Co., Ltd., 1958), p. 69]. In his revision of Wrenn's edition [Beowulf With the Finnesburg Fragment (New York: St. Martin's Press, 1973)], Whitney F. Bolton restores the lines to their manuscript position, but in his footnote he restates Wrenn's point that the lines "probably have been misplaced in the MS. from their proper position between 110 and 111. They are probably an amplification--whether by the poet himself or a later interpolator--of the account of the banishment of Cain ending at 110: and if restored to their proper place in the text would make good sense" (p. 104). I, however, am interested in looking at the text as it is available to readers of the manuscript, and I submit that the lines in question are applicable to the description of Grendel, a member of "Caines cynne."

[42] Joseph of Arimathea, De Transitu Beatae Mariae Virginis, in Apocalypses Apocryphae, ed. Konstantine von Tischendorf (Hildeshein: Georg Olms Verlagsbuchhandlung, 1966), p. 118.

[43] J. D. A. Ogilvy, Books Known to the English, 597-1066 (Cambridge, Mass.: Mediaeval Academy of America, 1967), p. 70.

[44] Assumptio S. Mariae Virginis, in The Blickling Homilies of the Tenth Century, ed. and trans. R. Morris, EETS, Old Series vols. 58, 63, and 73 (London: The Early English Text Society, 1880), p. 155.

[45] The theme of exile has been discussed by Stanley B. Greenfield, "The Formulaic Expression of the Theme of 'Exile' in Anglo-Saxon Poetry," Speculum, 30 (1955), pp. 200-6.

[46] The devils are, for example, called "wræcmæcgas" (l. 231b) [exiled persons] who inhabit "wræcsetla fela" (l. 296b) [many places of exile] and who live "in wræcsiðe" (l. 623b) [on the journey of exile]. After he defeats the exiled devils, Guthlac is able to "eardes brucan" (l. 745b) [enjoy his home]. Heaven is a place where the blessed may be "eardfæst" (l. 786b) [secure in their home] after they have journeyed "to fæder eðle" (l. 801b) [to the homeland of the Father].

[47] Robert of Sicily, ll. 410 and 408, in The Middle English Metrical Romances, ed. Walter Hoyt French and Charles Brockway Hale (New York: Russell and Russell, Inc., 1964), vol. 2, p. 945.

[48] James David Mason, "Monsters with Human Voices: The Anthropomorphic Adversary of the Hero in Old English and Old Norse Literature" (Diss. Univ. of Tennessee, 1976), p. vi. All further references appear in the text; quotations are made by permission of Dr. Mason.

[49] John Bugge, "The Virgin Phoenix," MS, 38 (1976), p. 333.

[50] In Old English, "neroxnawong" is used to refer both to the Earthly Paradise--the Garden of Eden-- and to Heaven, as it is used in the thirteenth Blickling Homily quoted on p. 38. In Guthlac A and The Phoenix, it is used to refer to the Earthly Paradise from which mankind was banished after the Fall.

⁵¹This point is discussed by Renoir in "Roland's Lament: Its Meaning and Function in the Chanson de Roland," Speculum, 35 (1960), pp. 572-83.

⁵²Felix, Life of St. Guthlac, ed. and trans. Bertram Colgrave (Cambridge: The Univ. Press, 1956). All references appear in the text; all translations are mine. In The Guthlac Poems, pp. 1-12, Roberts discusses the historicity of Guthlac and facts which are found in the Vita and The Anglo-Saxon Chronicle and charters.

⁵³Mircea Eliade, The Myth of the Eternal Return, or, Cosmos and History, trans. Willard R. Trask, Bollingen Series 46 (Princeton, New Jersey: Princeton Univ. Press, 1974), pp. 42-43. All further references appear in the text.

⁵⁴Although many critics, as typified by Gordon Hall Gerould in "The Old English Poems on St. Guthlac and Their Latin Source," MLN, 32 (1917), pp. 77-89, argue that Guthlac A must be dependent on Felix's Vita, Roberts has shown that whether the Vita "was used by the Guthlac A poet remains a problem open to debate" [The Guthlac Poems, p. 11]. Some modern critics assert that Guthlac A derives only from oral traditions about Guthlac. Kemp Malone, for example, states emphatically that the "author owed little if anything to Felix but relied on oral tradition, though making use of literary sources in giving literary form to this tradition" [The Middle Ages: The Old English Period, A Literary History of England, vol. 1, ed. Albert C. Baugh (New York: Appleton-Century-Crofts, 1967), p. 75]. In "The Structure and Background of Guthlac A" (Diss. Fordham Univ., 1972), Chester Kobos concludes that Guthlac A must be based on oral traditions because the poet says that the story was "told to him by a holy cleric or perhaps 'the holy clergy' (halig had). . . . [By saying] 'men often heard' (hyrdon) . . . he acknowledges that stories about Guthlac were part of the oral tradition" (pp. 1-3). Both phrases, however, can bear a different interpretation. As scholars like Jones

and Colgrave have pointed out, the most common way
in which stories about the saints "gewearð / þurh
haligne had gecyþed" (ll. 93b-94b) [were made known
by the holy order] was as products of the monastic
scriptorium read in the refectory or during liturgical services. I should like to suggest, therefore, that when the poet says "we hyrdon oft"
(l. 108a) [we often heard] he is referring to works
like Felix's Vita Guthlaci or the Old English adaptations thereof read in the monastery. In contrast
to Roberts, who asserts that Guthlac A gives "no
indications that the poet followed any part of the
Vita closely" [The Guthlac Poems, p. 29], Cornell
has examined both Guthlac A and the Vita closely
and adduced convincing evidence to show the dependence of the former on the latter, and I should like
to add a piece of evidence which I believe supports
her argument. As Hanning has pointed out, "precise
chronological indications of any kind are usually
lacking" in hagiography ["Beowulf as Heroic
History," Medievalia et Humanistica, Series 2, 5
(1974), p. 83]. Therefore, not even a hagiographer's statement that a saint lived in the
writer's own time is necessarily trustworthy. For
example, the translator of Felix's Vita whose work
is found in MS Cotton Vespasian D.xxi translated
even Felix's prologue, which is addressed to
Ælfwald, King of East Anglia, "who ruled from about
713 to 749" (Felix, Life of Guthlac, p. 15). Since
the work is a careful translation of the Vita made
in the early tenth century, two hundred years after
Ælfwald's death, it cannot be based on the testimony which "dihteras sædon" [informants said]
[Charles Wycliffe Goodwin, ed. and trans., The
Anglo-Saxon Version of the Life of St. Guthlac,
Hermit of Croyland (London: John Russell Smith,
1848), p. 5]. Referring to Guthlac A's deviations
from the Vita, Cornell says that "since there is
no trace of an alternative literary or oral tradition of Guthlaciana from which the poem could have
derived these materials . . . it is only logical
to conclude that the known tradition is most probably the original tradition and the one upon which
the poem is based" (p. 40). In the absence of con-

vincing evidence for the existence of an alternative tradition, I am acting on the assumption that the Guthlac A poet probably knew the Vita.

[55] Michael N. Nagler, Spontaneity and Tradition: A Study in the Oral Art of Homer (Berkeley, Los Angeles, and London: Univ. of California Press, 1974), p. 131. All further references appear in the text.

[56] Vladimir Propp, Morphology of the Folktale, trans. Laurence Scott, rev. Louis A. Wagner (Austin and London: Univ. of Texas Press, 1975), p. 36.

[57] Greenfield, A Critical History of Old English Literature, 2nd. printing (New York: New York Univ. Press, 1968), p. 120.

[58] Passages that show the saint's relationship to animals occur in many Latin hagiographic works, including the Vita Guthlaci. Such passages demonstrate the sanctity of the hero-saint; Bede says in the Vita Cuthberti, "Qui enim auctori omnium creaturarum fideliter et integro corde famulatur, non est mirandum si eius imperiis ac uotis omnis creatura deseruiat. At nos plerunque iccirco subiectae nobis creaturae dominium perdimus, quia Domino et creatori omnium ipsi seruire negligimus" (pp. 224-25) [For if a man faithfully and wholeheartedly serves the maker of all created things, it is no wonder though all creation should minister to his commands and wishes. But for the most part we lose dominion over the creation which was made subject to us, because we ourselves neglect to serve the Lord and Creator of all things]. However, such lyrical passages about the natural world do not occur in the extant Old English hagiographic poems except Guthlac A.

[59] Benedict, Abbot of Monte Cassino, The Rule, Commentary on the Holy Rule of St. Benedict, ed. and trans. Dom Justin McCann, 2nd ed. (London: Burns and Oates, 1959), p. 3.

[60] Shook, "Prologue," p. 302.

[61] Calder, "Theme and Strategy in *Guthlac B*," *PLL*, 8 (1972), p. 227.

[62] Adrien Bonjour, "*Beowulf* and the Beasts of Battle," *PMLA*, 72 (1957), p. 566. All further references appear in the text.

[63] Dante Alighieri, *The Divine Comedy: Paradiso*, vol. 1, ed. and trans. Charles S. Singleton, Bollingen Series, vol. 80 (Princeton, New Jersey: Princeton Univ. Press, 1975), pp. 380-81. The translation used is that of Singleton.

Chapter Three
Guthlac B and the Cycle of History

Section A
The Orosian View of Christian History

Like Guthlac A, Guthlac B has usually received
what Calder has described as "mechanical criticism
which scarcely accounts for the poem's real value."[1]
Early critics praised Guthlac B primarily because
there was a belief, to quote Anderson, that it
"shows marked resemblances to the four signed poems
of Cynewulf" (p. 136). Although no one now attributes Cynewulfian authorship to it, critics praise
its use of the traditional formulas, themes, and
type-scenes of Old English poetry, as may be exemplified by Theodor Wolpers' praise of its "Ver-
deutlichung des Geschehens durch kleinere, hoch-
emotionale und von affektischen Gebärden bestimmte
Teilszenen" (p. 118) and by Greenfield's praise of
its "Cynewulfian elaborations and poetic power" and
its use of the "Christian death theme [which] is
developed in Anglo-Saxon poetic fashion, as death
is presented in a series of sharp vignettes as it
advances upon the saint."[2]

Despite their almost universal admiration for
Guthlac B's verbal beauty and moving account of
Guthlac's death, critics have often argued that
the poem is inept because it fails to meet the
approved modern canons of narrative unity. Guthlac
B appears to have a disjunctive structure, for the
first third of the extant poem is devoted to the
Creation and Fall, whereas the remainder turns
without any apparent reason or transition to the
story of Guthlac's death and ends with the lament
of his disciple. Interpretation is rendered
especially difficult by the fact that the end of
the poem has been lost, so that each reader must
supply his own conclusion. We may reasonably
suppose, however, that a poet who is able to use
the ornamental details of his art as well as this
one does is likely to be sufficiently adept to use

its larger structures and themes coherently and with purpose. My contention is that the Guthlac B poet chooses both large and small details with skill and poetic judgment and composes a self-contained, circular narrative which distorts linear time rather than one with a temporal beginning, middle, and end. As mentioned in the first chapter, Old English poems tend to be static structures rather than sequential narratives, and Guthlac B's distortion of linear time is reminiscent of that of Beowulf.

Like many hagiographic works, Guthlac B has been improperly classified. James L. Rosier, for example, describes it as "typical of Lives in the tradition of the Vita Antonii,"[3] that is, those "instructive biographies . . . methodical [and] complete,"[4] which describe a saint's birth, conversion from the world, and holy death. Guthlac B should not, however, be considered an example of Antonian hagiography, for, as Woolf has pointed out, "the saint's life . . . is mentioned only in a brief introductory summary" (p. 57), and the poem concentrates on three subjects: The Fall of Man, the death of Guthlac, and the grief of his disciple. I suspect that critics insist on attempting to fit Guthlac B into the Antonian model primarily because Felix's Vita, on which it is based, is undeniably Antonian, even though many are aware that "the poem is indeed no slavish translation. . . . The poet recast structure, changed strategy, emphasized certain individual themes, introduced new strands of imagery, and augmented his tale beyond the restrictions of his source material."[5] Nevertheless, Rosier claims that Guthlac B concentrates on Guthlac's death in a way which is "to be expected, given the prominence of the saint's death in Antonian hagiography" (p. 82), although such emphasis is actually more reminiscent of the Patristic Passiones than of the Vita Antonii. Because Rosier believes that Guthlac B is Antonian, he dismisses the material on the Creation and Fall as merely "a full-scale prologue . . . [based on] Felix's brief, three-sentence introduction to Chapter L" (p. 85) which has little or no relevance to the actual subject of the poem. Anderson describes the material as "a brief account of the fall of man" (p. 136), and, like Rosier, he argues that the story of the Fall has no organic relevance to that of Guthlac's death and only a very slight relationship to other themes developed in the poem.

Although critics have praised the craftsmanship of Guthlac B, their belief that its first 178 lines contain irrelevant material implies that the author was inept. The long Old English poems have beginnings which make general statements exemplified in the rest of the poem. The opening of Beowulf, for example, introduces a theme which the poem explores at length, that of the way in which "æþelingas ellen fremedon" (l. 3) [noblemen performed deeds of valor], even though the deeds are not those of the Danes of the opening lines. Even the most clearly literary Old English poems are in a way successors of those composed in the oral tradition of the Germanic peoples. As a result, it is not surprising that they have strong beginnings which introduce important themes, for the beginning of an oral poem is its most frequently recited portion and is consequently relatively stable and well-developed.[6] Those critics, therefore, who say that the relationship between the beginning of Guthlac B and its central portion is only one of "implied associations"[7] are making a value judgment based on misinterpretation of the nature of a poem from a formulaic tradition.

Guthlac B is, to quote Rosier, "a self-contained expansion" (p. 82) of one chapter of Felix's Vita which includes few incidents from the remainder of the Vita's narrative about Guthlac's life and posthumous miracles but which does, as Langen's study of its imagery has shown, use image clusters not found in the Vita. Because of Guthlac B's close relationship to the Vita's description of Guthlac's death, however, critics like Wolpers emphasize that it is "eine erzählliedhaft verlebendigende Darstellung des Sterbens des Heiligen" (p. 115). Most critics also discuss some secondary, but related, theme: Greenfield the "relationship between Guthlac and his 'thane',"[8] Rosier the apotheosis of Guthlac, and Calder "the loss of beauty as a consequence of sin--which, in fact, combines with the topos of death as a separation to create a wholly original, though devoutly Christian, poetic statement."[9] One may argue, however, that the poem is not merely an expansion of one brief chapter of the Vita showing what Woolf calls "complexity and range of feeling" (p. 57) but is, instead, about a different subject: the Fall and Redemption of man as exemplified in Guthlac's life. All interpretations which regard Guthlac B as simply an expansion of material of the Vita exemplifying the latter's Antonian spirit ignore the fact that the first third of the extant poem explores not the story of Guthlac but that of Adam and Eve. Furthermore, dismissal of the material on the Creation and Fall as merely a "prologue" which is more or less irrelevant to the remainder of the poem seems to echo the words of the Friar in the Canterbury Tales: "'Now dame,' quod he, 'so have I joye or blis, / This is a long preamble of a tale.'"[10] Like the "long preamble" of the Wife of Bath's Tale, that of Guthlac B turns out to be fully relevant to the tale which follows.

I have suggested that "there are grounds for arguing that the poem reflects the influence of Orosius' Historiarum Adversum Paganos Libri Septem,"[11] and I believe that Guthlac B can be coherently interpreted as a complete unit if we assume that it was influenced by the view of history expressed by Orosius rather than that expressed by St. Augustine in De Civitate Dei. In contrast to Augustine, Orosius describes history as a recurrent cycle of events in which it is possible to discern both God's judgments and His purpose, and in this recurrent cycle the only difference between Christians and their pagan ancestors is that the pagans lived before the Incarnation and did not have access to the means of salvation. Orosius says that "quisquis per se atque in se humanum genus uidet"[12] [everyone sees the human race through himself and in himself] and that each man re-enacts the history of mankind briefly in his own life, especially the crucial events of Fall and Redemption. As a result, the life history of each individual human being can best be understood through its resemblance to the history of all mankind.

Although Guthlac B is undeniably close in subject matter to the Vita Guthlaci, its tone and philosophical attitude are utterly different from the Augustinian ones of Felix's careful adaptation of the Vita Antonii, which describes the spiritual pilgrimage of Guthlac after he leaves the City of Man for the City of God found in his hermitage. Unlike Athanasius or Augustine, Orosius is uninterested in the story of the inner spiritual journey of a particular human being; instead, he is concerned with the means whereby individual lives fit into the recurring patterns of Fall and Redemption which comprise the history of mankind. Guthlac B describes both cyclical patterns, and the first starts at the beginning of the history of mankind when "þone ærestan ælda cynnes / of þære clænestan, cyning ælmihtig, / foldan geworhte" (ll. 821a-23a) [the Almighty King made the first of the race of men from the purest earth]. The Libri Septem opens at the beginning of human history, for its purpose is "initium miseriae hominum ab initio peccati hominis ducere" (p. 6) [to consider the beginning of the miseries of men from the beginning of the sin of man], and Guthlac B also traces human misery from the Fall. Both the Libri Septem and Guthlac B concentrate on describing the effects of the Fall and the miseries of mankind, for, as the former says, after "humanum genus libidinibus deprauatum peccatis obsorduisset, continuo iniustam licentiam iusta punitio consecuta est" (p. 40) [the human race, depraved by lusts, became filthy with sins, a just punishment at once followed unjust license]. The Libri Septem does not describe that Paradise "quem rectum atque immaculatum fecerat Deus" (p. 40) [which God made upright and immaculate], and Guthlac B describes Adam's prelapsarian life in Paradise purely in terms of the absence of the miseries with which God punished sinful man, that is, sorrow, aging, and death:

73

> Þær him nænges wæs
> willan onsyn   ne welan brosnung
> ne lifes lyre   ne lices hryre
> ne dreames dryre   ne deaðes cyme
> ac he on þam lande   lifgan moste
> ealra leahtra leas,   longe neotan
> niwra gefeana;   þær he no þorfte
> lifes ne lissa   in þam leohtan ham
> þurh ælda tid   ende gebidan.
>   (ll. 827b-35b)

[There was for him the lack of no desire, no decay of happiness, no loss of life, no decay of the body, no cessation of joy, and no coming of death, but he might live in that land completely sinless and enjoy new joys for a long time; there in that bright home he did not need to await the end of life and delight during the time of old age.]

Many critics have pointed out that the negative description of Paradise is conventional in Christian literature and have mentioned the Old English Phoenix as another work which uses it. The Phoenix, however, firmly establishes the positive aspects of Paradise and describes it as "wlitig" (l. 7a) [fair], "ænlic" (l. 9a) [unique], and "wynnum geblissad" (l. 7b) [blessed with joys]. The second part of The Phoenix's description of Paradise is negative, but it limits the negative aspects of the Fall to the effect thereof on the weather:

> Ne mæg þær ren ne snaw
> ne forstes fnæst   ne fyres blæst
> ne hægles hryre   ne hrimes dryre
> ne sunnan hætu   ne sincaldu
> ne wearm weder   ne winterscur
> wihte gewyrdan.
>   (ll. 14b-19a)

[Neither rain nor snow, nor the breath of the frost, nor the blast of the fire, nor the fall of the hail, nor the downpour of

> the rime-frost, nor the heat of the sun,
> nor perpetual cold, nor warm weather, nor
> winter showers, in any way may cause
> damage there.]

In contrast to the sorrowful description of Paradise in Guthlac B, that in The Phoenix is idyllic, for it emphasizes the positive aspects of "neorxnawong." Like the Libri Septem, Guthlac B emphasizes two points: human sorrows and the effects of the Fall on men. It mentions the miseries of Adam and Eve who "scofene wurdon / on gewinworuld" (ll. 856b-57a) [were thrust into a world of care], of Guthlac, who dies and leaves a world where "he blædes . . . brucan moste, / worulde lifes" (ll. 931a-32a) [he was permitted to enjoy happiness, the life of the world], and of the disciple, left desolate by Guthlac's death.

Guthlac B speaks of the Fall very briefly: Adam and Eve eat a "deaðberende gyfl / þæt ða sinhiwan to swylte geteah" (ll. 850b-51b) [death-bearing morsel which led the wedded couple to death]. The description is not dramatic and occupies only seven and one-half lines. Guthlac B then omits the dismissal scene and skips directly to the first effect of the Fall, man's loss of Paradise:

> Siþþan se eþel uðgenge wearð
> Adame 7 Euan, eardwica cyst,
> beorht, oðbroden.
> (ll. 852a-54a)

> [Afterwards, the homeland passed out of
> the possession of Adam and Eve, the bright
> best of dwelling-places was taken away.]

In this episode, Guthlac B eliminates the drama of the traditional story, for Adam and Eve are not driven out of the garden by an angel with a flaming sword; in fact, they do not even leave Paradise, but it is taken away from them. As may be exemplified by Genesis B, Old English poetry can movingly express the drama of the Fall, the temptation of Adam and Eve by the serpent and their confrontation with God. In contrast, Guthlac B mentions only those points of the story which are pertinent to its theme and help establish its Orosian tone. The Libri Septem omits any description of the Temptation and Fall, for Orosius' purpose is to emphasize the effects of the Fall on mankind. It repeatedly emphasizes the inevitable and inescapable effects of men's actions and the fact that glory and happiness abandon them, and it lists various historical figures who had everything of worldly value, lost it, and died miserably, but it does not describe their stories in dramatic terms. Like the Libri Septem, Guthlac B suggests that no one can escape the repeated pattern of the Fall of Man, and in order to understand why Guthlac must live in exile, suffer, and die, we must understand the Fall, because Guthlac suffers and dies "swa him biforan worhton / þa ærestan ælda cynnes" (ll. 974b-75b) [as the first of the race of men did before him]. The first 178 lines of the poem accordingly concentrate on Adam and Eve and all their descendants, who are typified by Guthlac and his disciple; they are, therefore, an essential part of Guthlac B.

    Guthlac B states that the most important consequence of the Fall is that Death "in geþrong / fira cynne, feond rixade / geond middangeard" (ll. 863b-65a) [pressed in upon the race of men, the enemy ruled throughout the world]. Although all Christian writers agree that death entered the world as a punishment for Adam's sin, the Libri Septem places a special emphasis on the fact that Death is the ruler of the post-lapsarian world. For example, it describes how the powerful and well-fortified city of Babylon "uicta, capta, subuersa est" (p. 97) [was conquered, captured, and overthrown] by Cyrus, who shortly thereafter was slain by the Scythian queen Thamyris. Guthlac B also shows that man is helpless to avert his death and cannot turn away from "þone bitran drync / þone Eue fyrn Adame geaf" (ll. 868b-69b) [the bitter drink which Eve formerly gave to Adam]. One of the men whom the Libri Septem describes as "godes willan . . . georn is Athaulf, King of the Goths, an exemplar of kingly virtues, "Romanae restitutionis auctor, . . . [qui] abstinere a bello . . . [et] inhiare paci nitebatur" (p. 560) [the author of the restoration of Rome, who strove to refrain from war and to be eager for peace]. Even so just a man could not avert his death, for "apud Barcinonam Hispaniae urbem dolo suorum . . . occisus est" (p. 561) [in the city of Barcelona in Spain, he was slain by the treachery of his own men].

Guthlac B turns to Guthlac himself only after describing the Fall and emphasizing that "Deað ricsade / ofer foldbuend" (ll. 871b-72a) [Death has ruled over the earth-dwellers], and it says that Guthlac is one of those men who is "gæsthaligra" (l. 873a) [holy in spirit] and serves God. It moves from its general statement about fallen humanity to the specific case of Guthlac by a temporal, transitional half-line, "æfter tælmearce" (l. 877a) [at a later period], which suggests the Orosian view that the cycle of human events is continuously repeated. The poem describes Guthlac as distant from its audience in time and known only from "bec" (l. 878b) [books]. The Libri Septem likewise emphasizes that it is describing the history of the world as found in books, for it speaks of "omnes propemodum tam apud Graecos quam apud Latinos studiosi ad scribendum uiri, qui res gestas regum populorumque ob diuturnam memoriam uerbis propagauerunt" (p. 5) [almost all men, among both the Greeks and the Latins, interested in writing, who have perpetuated in words the deeds of kings and peoples for a lasting record of the past].

Guthlac B presents Guthlac as a famous and powerful man, like those described in the Libri Septem. It emphasizes the fact that "his wundra geweorc" (l. 882a) [his works of miracles] are "breme æfter burgum geond Bryten innan" (l. 883) [renowned among the cities throughout Britain]. Like the people in the Libri Septem, however, Guthlac suffers tribulation. Just as Adam and Eve were tempted to sin "þurh deofles searo" (l. 850a) [through a trick of the devil], so Guthlac is persecuted by "deofla deaðmægen" (l. 895a) [a deadly band of devils]. As Calder points out, the description of the devils is "a series that reflects back upon the earlier description of Eden and the results of Adam's fall,"[13] although one should note that the devils have been afflicted with all the miseries which are absent in Paradise. The devils are fallen beyond all hope of redemption and show all the evil effects of the Fall, being "wrohtsmiðas" (l. 905a) [workers of crime], "earmra gæsta" (l. 904a) [rather miserable spirits], and "hiwes binotene, / dreamum bidrorene" (ll. 900b-1a) [bereft of beauty, deprived of joys]. They epitomize the Orosian picture of human existence: miserable, chaotic, and constantly filled with war. The <u>Libri</u> <u>Septem</u> says that the "bella cladesque" (p. 7) [wars and disasters] which afflict mankind "aut manifesta peccata sunt aut occultae punitiones peccatorum" (pp. 7-8) [are either manifest sins or the hidden punishments of sins], and <u>Guthlac B</u> describes devils who are "weorude" (l. 894b) [in a host] and call out "hludne herecirm" (l. 900a) [with a loud war-cry]. Guthlac also is a warrior in the fallen world, for he is "dryhtnes cempa, / from folctoga" (ll. 901b-2a) [the champion of the Lord, the bold leader of the people] who resists valiantly "feonda þreatum" (l. 902b) [the troops of the enemies].

Old English hagiographic poems often apply the language of heroic poetry to their descriptions of saints in order to compare the old heroic world and the new one of God's warriors. Critics have been tempted to view <u>Guthlac B</u>'s use of such language as, in Cherniss' words, "mechanical and largely gratuitous" (p. 241) because it differs from that of other poems. However, it is used to emphasize the warlike nature of the fallen world which neither good nor evil persons can escape and is, therefore, necessary to establish the Orosian tone. <u>Guthlac B</u> also characterizes the devils by their inhuman appearance and constant noise, recalling the <u>Libri</u> <u>Septem</u>'s emphasis on the chaos, tumult, and dehumanization of the world. When the devils attack Guthlac, they take three different forms:

> Hwilum wedende   swa wilde deor
> cirmdon on corðre,   hwilum cyrdon eft
> minne mansceaþan   on mennisc hiw
> breahtma mæste,   hwilum brugdon eft
> awyrgde wærlogan   on wyrmes bleo,
> earme adloman,   attre spiowdon.
>   (ll. 907a-12b)

[Sometimes, raging like wild beasts, they clamored in a band, sometimes the vile evil foes changed again into human form with the greatest of tumults, sometimes the accursed oathbreakers turned again into the form of serpents, and the wretched ones, crippled by fire, spewed out poison.]

Guthlac B uses eight different expressions within twenty-two lines to characterize the devils' chaotic noise. In contrast to the Vita Guthlaci's Antonian presentation of the attacks of the devils as psychological stages in Guthlac's eremitical life, Guthlac B describes them briefly in a way that epitomizes the misery of the fallen world.[14] The devils are actually powerless to injure Guthlac, for they can only threaten him with "feorhcwealm" (l. 915b) [the pain of death], and Guthlac, a descendant of Adam, cannot hope to escape death because it is the legacy of the Fall.

After the devils threaten Guthlac with death, Guthlac B turns to a description of it. As Rosier says, "the poet personifies Death . . . [as] a trespasser or alien warrior who seeks to enter, to unlock, the saint's domain . . . and plunder the treasure" (p. 86). He does not, however, note how often the passive voice is used in Guthlac B, which describes death less as a vivid, personified actor than as an agent. Although "Deað in geþrong / fira cynne" (ll. 863b-64a) [Death pressed in upon the race of men] after the Fall, and although "færinga / adl in gewod" (ll. 939b-40a) [sickness moved quickly in on] Guthlac as he neared death, the personifications of both death and illness are less important than the description of their effects on men. Guthlac B emphasizes the effect of Guthlac's illness as the Libri Septem emphasizes that of war and pestilence, for Guthlac's "breosthord onboren [is]" (l. 944a) [breasthoard is weakened], his body is "adle onæled" (l. 955a) [consumed by disease], and his "lichord onlocen [is]" (l. 956a) [hoard of the body is unlocked]. The Orosian study of the Fall of Man in Guthlac B ends with the statement that Guthlac faces the penalty assigned to Adam and Eve "7 hyra bearnum" (l. 854b) [and their children], death:

> Wæs neah seo tid
> þæt he fyrngewyrht   fyllan sceolde
> þurh deaðes cyme,   domes hleotan,
> efne þæs ilcan   þe usse yldran fyrn
> frecne onfengon.
> (ll. 970b-74a)

[The time was near when he had to fulfill the ancient decree through the coming of death, obtain by lot his judgment, even that same one which our ancestors boldly received long ago.]

The second Orosian cyclical pattern, that of the Redemption, begins in the middle of Guthlac B's description of the cycle of the Fall, just as it does in the Libri Septem, which describes the birth of Christ in the middle of its recital of the miseries of fallen man:

> Natus est Christus salutarem mundo adferens fidem, uere petra medio rerum posita, ubi comminueretur qui offenderet, qui crederet saluaretur; uere ignis ardens, quem qui sequitur inluminatur, qui temptat exuritur; ipse est Christus, Christianorum caput, saluator bonorum, malorum punitor, iudex omnium, qui formam subsecuturis uerbo et opere statuens.
> (pp. 437-38)

[Christ was born, bringing the saving faith to the world, truly, the rock placed in the middle of things, where he who knocks

against it will be broken into small pieces,
but he who believes will be saved; truly, a
burning fire, which illuminates him who
follows it, which consumes entirely him who
attacks it; He Himself is the Christ, the
Head of Christians, the Savior of the good,
Who stands in word and deed as the type
of His followers.]

The <u>Libri Septem</u> does not tell the traditional
story of the Fall, nor does it relate the story of
the Incarnation, discussing instead the effect
thereof on men. <u>Guthlac B</u> likewise is interested
not in the story of the Incarnation but in its
effect on those men, as exemplified by Guthlac,
who re-live its pattern in their own lives and
choose for themselves eternal "meaht 7 mundbyrd"
(l. 881a) [might and protection]. In <u>Guthlac B</u>
Christ is indeed "formam subsecuturis"; in fact,
Guthlac is described as being so like Christ that
he was born to fulfill the Redemptive cycle. The
lines which describe his likeness to Christ are
emphatically not in keeping with the ideas of
Augustine, who constantly stresses "the uniqueness
of the scriptural record."[15] Like Christ, Guthlac
was "acennedne þurh cildes had / gumena cynnes to
Godes dome, / werigra wraþu" (ll. 1361a-63a) [born
in the form of a child of the race of men by the
decree of God, the help of the weary]. Guthlac so
well relives the redemptive pattern in his own life,
both "uerbo et opere," that he becomes Christ to
his fellow men and heals the disastrous effects of
the Fall upon their lives; in fact, he heals both
"lic 7 sawle" (l. 929a) [body and soul]. Guthlac
also aids the "fugla cyn" (l. 917a) [race of birds]
who, like the rest of the natural world, share the
fallen condition with mankind, and he feeds them
when they come to him, "hungre geþreatad" (l. 916b)
[urged by hunger]. As a symbol of the unity of
man and nature, the birds honor him "meaglum
stefnum" (l. 919a) [with earnest voices].

Although Guthlac is able to heal the effects
of the Fall in the lives of other men and the birds,
he must nevertheless face death himself, for even

Christ had to die. Guthlac, "elnes anhydig" (l. 978a) [steadfast of valor], follows the teaching of Christ, Who, in the words of the Libri Septem, exhorts His followers to be "patientes in persecutionibus, quas pro vita æterna exciperent" (p. 438) [patient in the persecutions, which they would endure for the sake of eternal life]. Guthlac B's description of Guthlac's death begins with a reminder that he, like all men, is following the cycle of the Fall which ends with his own death. However, since he dies in the era of the Redemption and has re-enacted Christ's life in his own, Guthlac has no need to fear the "bryþen . . . / þætte Adame Eue gebyrmde / æt fruman worulde" (ll. 980b-82a) [drink which Eve brewed for Adam at the beginning of the world]. It is logical that the Orosian Guthlac B should describe Eve's legacy to mankind in imagery associated with drinking, because the Libri Septem describes many incidents of bloodshed in terms of drinking. For example, it says that Ninus, King of Assyria, first taught mankind to wage war: "Scythiamque barbariem, adhuc tunc inbellem et innocentem, torpentem excitare saeuitiam, uires suas nosse, et non lacte iam pecudum sed sanguinem hominum bibere . . . edocuit" (pp. 42-43) [He taught barbaric Scythia, until then peaceful and innocent, to arouse its inert ferocity, to understand its strength, and to drink not the milk of cattle but the blood of men].

Guthlac B now introduces another character, Guthlac's "ombehtþegn" (l. 1000a) [attendant], nameless in the poem, although critics habitually give him the name of Beccel, which "is gleaned from Felix."[16] Since the poem is a translation of a chapter of the Vita Guthlaci, its author must have been acquainted with the name of Guthlac's servant and have deliberately chosen not to name him. Guthlac B does not, in fact, present even Guthlac as a vividly personified character, but merely as a typical human being whose life demonstrates the effects of the Fall and the Redemption. It may have therefore withheld the well-known name of Guthlac's disciple in order to make the "ombehtþegn" less vividly personified than the Vita's Beccel, with whom certain specific actions are associated, such as his attempt, when unable to withstand the temptations of the devil, to murder Guthlac. Guthlac B makes the disciple a general representative of fallen humanity and explores the effects of Guthlac's illness and death on him just as it earlier explored the effects of the Fall on Adam and Eve and their descendants. As soon as the disciple perceives that Guthlac is ill, "him ðæt in gefeol / hefig æt heortan" (ll. 1008b-9a) [heaviness fell upon his heart], a statement that echoes the earlier comment that, after the Fall, Death "in geþrong" (l. 863b) [pressed in upon] mankind. Guthlac B places equal emphasis on the themes of Guthlac's death and of its effect on the disciple, in contrast to the Vita, which concentrates on Guthlac's death and only briefly mentions Beccel's grief: "Praedictus frater flens et gemens crebris lacrimarum rivulis maestas genas rigavit. Quem vir Dei consolans ait . . ." (p. 154) [The brother mentioned before, weeping and sighing, moistened his sorrowful cheeks with frequent rivulets of tears. The man of God consoling him said . . .]. The difference between Guthlac and his disciple lies specifically in the fact that Guthlac has been re-enacting the Redemption in his life, whereas his disciple is still re-enacting the Fall.

Guthlac is suffering from the effects of the Fall and is "adlwerigne" (l. 1008a) [weary from illness] because he is as helpless as Adam and Eve to escape his fate. Like the Libri Septem, Guthlac B emphasizes that happiness and worldly pleasure inevitably abandon men, and it emphasizes, therefore, the end of the time when Guthlac "blædes her brucan moste, / worulde lifes" (ll. 931a-32a) [was permitted to enjoy here happiness, the life of the world]. Thus, although the onset of Guthlac's final illness is a joyful event because he is confident that he will go to Heaven, it also ambiguously heralds his departure from this joyful world. This view of the world as a place of mingled joy and sorrow which we are both glad and sorry to leave is Orosian rather than Augustinian, for the

Libri Septem describes the way in which the same events can be considered both good and evil: "Ecce quam feliciter Roma uincit tam infeliciter quidquid extra Romam est uincitur. Quanti igitur pendenda est gutta haec laboriosae felicitatis, cui adscribitur unius urbis beatitudo in tanta mole infelicitatis, per quam agitur totius Orbis euersio?" (pp. 276-77) [Behold, how happily Rome conquers, so that whatever is outside Rome is unhappily conquered. Therefore, how heavily is this drop of laborious happiness to be weighed, to which the happiness of one city is to be attributed among so much unhappiness, through which the destruction of the whole world comes about?]. "Eadig on elne" (l. 1026a) [blessed in valor], Guthlac continues to re-enact the cycle of the Redemption, acting as Christ to his disciple. Guthlac tells his disciple that he will die within seven days and that he will "meorda hleotan, / gingra geafena" (ll. 1041b-42a) [obtain a reward, the joys of the disciples]. When his disciple seems inconsolable, Guthlac attempts to comfort him, bringing the Gospel so effectively to him that he plays the role of the Holy Spirit, the Comforter left after Christ's Ascension, and is, in fact, called "gæsta halig" (l. 1060a) [holy of spirit], a phrase which is reminiscent of the Old English name for the Holy Spirit, "Se Halga Gast."[17]

The language of Guthlac B is full of echoes from the Biblia Vulgata which reinforce the identification of Guthlac with Christ. In the case of well-known passages, it may be argued that the phrases were immediately meaningful to their intended audience and enhanced the impact of the poem, especially since some extant Old English Biblical translations use phraseology that resembles that of Guthlac B. Guthlac calls his disciple "min þæt leofe bearn" (l. 1076b) [my beloved son], just as Christ addresses both His disciples and those to whom He ministers as His children. In Mark 2:5, for example, Christ says to a paralyzed man, "Fili, dimittuntur tibi peccata tua," a passage which Ælfric renders as "Min bearn, ðe synd þine synna forgifene"[18] [My son, your sins are forgiven].

Guthlac dies during the Easter season; as has often been noted,[19] hagiographic literature describes many saints who follow the pattern of Christ's life so perfectly that they die at Easter. <u>Guthlac B</u>, however, emphasizes not the historical event of the Passion but its effect, the institution of the feast of Easter. <u>Guthlac B</u> mentions the Resurrection only in a modifying clause describing one day during Guthlac's final illness:

>   Þa se dæg bicwom
> on þam se lifgenda   in lichoman,
> ece ælmihtig   ærist gefremede,
> dryhten mid dreame,   ða he of deaðe aras,
> onwald of eorðan   in þa eastortid,
> ealra þrymma þrym   --ðreata mæstne
> to heofonum ahof,   ða he from helle astag.
>   (ll. 1098b-1104b)

[Then the day came on which the living, eternal, Almighty One, the Lord, joyfully performed His Resurrection in His body, when He arose from death, powerful from the earth in the season of Easter, the Glory of all Glories--He was carried to Heaven by the might of hosts, when He mounted up from Hell.]

Guthlac makes an offering "in Godes temple" (l. 1113b) [in the temple of God] and begins "þurh gæstes giefe   godspel bodian" (l. 1115) [to preach the Gospel through the grace of the Spirit]. He preaches so well that his disciple considers his sermon to be the word of "ufancundes   engles" (l. 1124) [an angel from above] rather than "æniges monnes lar / wera ofer eorðan" (ll. 1126b-27a) [the teaching of any man of the men on earth]. Guthlac has the "mod 7 mægencræft,   þe him meotud engla, / gæsta geocend,   forgiefen hæfde" (ll. 1132a-33b) [mind and strength, which the Maker of angels, the Savior of spirits, had given to him].

Guthlac B emphasizes repeatedly that Guthlac's painful death is, like the Libri Septem's "miseriae hominum" (p. 6) [miseries of men], a consequence of the Fall. Death, personified as a warrior attacking Guthlac "hildescurun" (l. 1143b) [with battle-showers], like the warlike devils earlier in the poem reminds us of the wars and tribulations of mankind described in the Libri Septem. The traditional heroic vocabulary of Old English poetry, used to personify death, reinforces the Orosian tone of the poem and emphasizes that the adverse effects of the Fall--misery, war, and death--are closely interrelated.

Just before Guthlac dies, he feeds himself with the "husle" (l. 1300b) [consecrated bread and wine], and after taking the Viaticum, he sends forth his spirit "weorcum wlitigne in wuldres dream" (l. 1304) [beautiful with good works into the joy of Heaven]. Since Communion is traditionally referred to as "Passionis . . . memoriam"[20] [the memorial of the Passion] which makes present the sacrifice and Redemption of Christ, it is fitting for Guthlac to die after taking Communion and thus complete the Redemptive cycle at the same time as he completes that of the Fall. Like Christ, Guthlac must die but will go to Heaven.

Critics who believe that Guthlac B is only concerned with describing the death of Guthlac likewise misinterpret the place that his actual death has in the poem. Calder, for example, says that "Guthlac's life ends with his transfiguration,"[21] and he considers that the account of the transfiguration is the climax of the poem. As a result, he virtually ignores the conclusion, which turns to Guthlac's disciple. Calder's emphasis on the importance of Guthlac's apotheosis would be more applicable to a discussion of Guthlac A, for the latter poem ends in Heaven and does not return to earth.

Within our extant poem, Guthlac's disciple never re-enacts the cycle of Redemption in his life, but only that of the Fall. When Guthlac reveals that his death is near, his disciple laments. His grief--"wop 7 heaf" (l. 1047b) [weeping and lamentation] and "geocor sefa, geomrende hyge" (l. 1048) [sad spirit, mourning mind]--reminds us of the incidents in the Libri Septem that recount the miseries of mankind. Like Guthlac's death or the miseries of mankind, the disciple's grief is inescapable because grief is one of the adverse effects of the Fall, and the disciple cannot have "onbæru" (l. 1054b) [self-restraint]. Guthlac, who is "glædmod, Gode leof" (l. 1062a) [cheerful in mind and dear to God], attempts to comfort "geomormodes / drusendne hyge" (ll. 1060b-61a) [the drooping mind of the sorrowful one]. He bids his disciple to rejoice because Guthlac is going "to þam longan gefean / in eadwelan" (ll. 1090b-91a) [to lasting joy in blessedness], and he then begins "godspel bodian" (l. 1115b) [to preach the Gospel].

Neither Guthlac's personal assurances nor the Word of God itself can comfort the disciple, for the Redemptive cycle can be re-enacted only by one who chooses to do so. As a result, when the disciple finds Guthlac dying, he is "hygegeomor, / freorig 7 ferðwerig" (ll. 1156b-57a) [sad in mind, chilled with sorrow, and soul-weary], despite Guthlac's admonition to carry out their "wære 7 winescype" (l. 1172a) [covenant and friendship]. The disciple's last request to Guthlac is that his master lighten his "hygesorge" (l. 1205a) [sorrow of mind]. The disciple is troubled because Guthlac has had an angelic visitor, and the poem suggests that he may be unable to accept the impingement of the supernatural world on the natural one and therefore fears it. Guthlac, who continues to re-enact the role of Christ in the poem, attempts to comfort his disciple by saying, "A ic sibbe wiþ þe / healdan wille" (ll. 1262b-63a) [I will always hold peace with you]. His statement echoes Christ's words to His disciples in John 14:27: "Pacem relinquo vobis, pacem meam do vobis," translated by Ælfric as "Ic forlæte eow sibbe; and ic forgife eow mine sybbe"[22] [I leave you my peace; my peace I give to you]. The echo of Biblical language once again reinforces the similarity which Guthlac B shows exists between Guthlac and Christ.

Before Guthlac dies, supernatural portents fill "þam halgan hofe" (1. 1147a) [the holy dwelling]: "Him of muðe cwom / swecca swetast" (ll. 1272a-73a) [The sweetest of odors came from his mouth] and "cwom leohta mæst, / halig of heofonum" (ll. 1282b-83a) [the greatest of lights, a holy one, came from Heaven]. The odor of sanctity and the heavenly light are commonplaces of hagiography and denote, as Langen says, "a virtuous life rewarded by physical incorruptibility" (p. 98), but Guthlac B also uses them, as Calder has noted, to compare "an ancient paradise lost . . . [with] a new paradise found."[2][3] However, Guthlac B does not merely contrast Adam, who disobeys God and loses Paradise, to Guthlac, who obeys Him and regains it, for the latter regains Paradise just at the time when he is suffering from miseries similar to those which did not exist in Paradise and is, therefore, like Adam after his Fall. By exploring how a man who has re-enacted Christ's Redemption in his life endures the miseries of the Fall "mægne modig" (1. 1272a) [brave in his strength] and is rewarded with divine favor, Guthlac B shows that there is no need for those who live in the era of Redemption to lament the way the disciple does. He, however, has not yet begun the redemptive cycle and is "afyrhted" (1. 1326b) [terrified] by the portents which accompany Guthlac's death.

Guthlac B does not describe Heaven but only states that the angelic hosts carry Guthlac's soul "to þam longan gefean" (1. 1307a) [to lasting joy], for the poem is concerned with this world. Furthermore, it does not merely describe the holy death and apotheosis of Guthlac, "Godes cempan" (1. 889a) [God's champion], a heroic figure whose life has been consciously modelled on Christ's. According to Orosius, not only the heroes of the Church but, indeed, everyone has the duty to re-enact in his own life the history of salvation since all of us have fallen like Adam and re-enact his Fall. Therefore, Guthlac B turns to the disciple who, like all

88

men, lives in the post-lapsarian world of exile, grief, and death and who is "elnes biloren" (l. 1327a) [bereft of courage] when he sees the angelic hosts and inconsolable because of Guthlac's death:

> Gnornsorge wæg
> hate æt heortan hygegeomurne,
> meðne modsefan, se þe his mondryhten
> life bilidene last weardian
> wiste wine leofne.
> (ll. 1335b-39a)

[He bore sorrow hot in his heart, sadness of mind, a weary spirit, he who knew that his lord, his beloved friend, remained behind him, deprived of life.]

The disciple leaves the island hermitage to fulfill Guthlac's last command and notify his master's sister of the latter's death. Guthlac B does not name the sister, although her name, St. Pega, is known from Felix's Vita Guthlaci and from other hagiographic works. By not naming her, Guthlac B makes her not one specific person whose holy life is well known but another general example, like Guthlac's nameless disciple, of a descendant of Adam and Eve. Guthlac B may have originally used Guthlac's sister either to demonstrate how the redemptive cycle is re-enacted in a life other than Guthlac's or to suggest that the cycle of Fall and Redemption is everlasting and exists in every human life. The extant poetic fragment suggests that her role is merely to remind the audience that the Orosian cycles exist beyond the confines of the poem because she is another person who has re-enacted the redemptive cycle.

Guthlac B ends with the disciple's "fusleoð" (l. 1346b) [death-song] which describes Guthlac's death as a sorrowful event even though Guthlac has gone "wica neosan, / eardes on upweg" (ll. 1365b-66a) [on the way to Heaven, to seek a dwelling, a home]. The last words of our extant text are the disciple's lament that he must "sarigferð / heanmod hweorfan hyge drusendne" (ll. 1378b-79b) [depart sorrowing in soul, dejected in spirit, with a drooping mind], a state of affairs which exactly parallels that at the beginning of the poem when Adam and Eve "scofene wurdon / on gewinworuld" (ll. 856b-57a) [were thrust into a world of care]. In this manner, the cycle of human history is being re-enacted in the life of a person who, like Guthlac, lives in the era of Redemption and has the obligation to re-enact in his life the history of salvation. At this point, the hiatus in the manuscript occurs.

All interpretations of <u>Guthlac B</u> have made surmises about the lost conclusion. R. T. Farrell has even suggested that <u>Azarias</u>, the poem which follows the missing section, may be the conclusion of <u>Guthlac B</u> and should "be taken as the praises uttered by Guthlac's sister, or . . . the songs sung by Guthlac's sister and retainer when they return to discover the odour of sanctity in Guthlac's place of death."[24] As Jane Roberts points out, however, "the grounds for demonstrating that the <u>Guthlac B</u> poet intended the <u>Azarias</u> songs to serve as an ending for his poem are weak . . . [and their] relevance to <u>Guthlac B</u> remains unproven."[25] Other critics have suggested that one or more folios, which contained the conclusion of <u>Guthlac</u>, the beginning of <u>Azarias</u>, and, perhaps, other poems, have been lost from between folios 52 and 53.[26] I do not intend to contribute to this discussion, because we do not need to believe that folios are missing in order to speculate that the original <u>Guthlac B</u> was longer than the extant poem, for many Old English poems have come to us in a fragmentary condition and lack either their beginnings or their conclusions. <u>Pharaoh</u>, for example, an eight-line poem in the <u>Exeter Book</u>, is probably a "fragment of a longer poem in dialogue form,"[27] and yet it was copied in such a way that it resembles the short poems which surround it.

On aesthetic grounds, however, many critics feel uncomfortable with the fragmentary condition of <u>Guthlac B</u>. Langen, for example, comments that "it does not seem possible that the poem was meant to end with the pronouncements of Beccel; the misery in them needs to be resolved" (p. 101). I am, however, tempted to believe that any writer who follows the history of the world as outlined in the Libri Septem must be influenced by the spirit of the work, which describes the history of mankind as full of unresolved misery. Woolf speculates that Guthlac B deliberately concludes with a "final elegiac effect [which] derives from the fact that the poem seems to end, not with the joyful description of Guthlac's soul being borne to Heaven by angels, but by the lament of his servant, who speaks in the role of the bereaved retainer" (p. 58). My own view is that the "elegiac effect" is Orosian rather than Augustinian, for Orosius views the inevitable downfall and death of even the wicked as pathetic, whereas Augustine views them as simply the just judgments of God. The spirit of the Libri Septem is obviously compatible with the mood of much extant Old English poetry, which may be summed up by a well-known statement from The Wanderer:

> Her bið feoh læne, her bið freond læne,
> her bið mon læne, her bið mæg læne,
> eal þis eorþan gesteal idel weorþeð!
> (ll. 108a-10b)

> [Here treasure is transitory, here a friend is transitory; here man is transitory, here woman is transitory; all the foundation of the world becomes useless.]

The elegiac effect of the passage describing Guthlac's death is heightened by its mention of Adam's Fall and its reminder that death is the penalty for sin, so that the passage is a lament both for the death of Guthlac and for man's loss of innocence and Paradise. Woolf expresses some surprise that in Guthlac B "the Anglo-Saxon melancholy sensitivity to transience and the Christian confidence in the Resurrection . . . [are not] poetically irreconcilable" (p. 58), but given the Orosian nature of the poem, the reconciliation of

these two ideas is only to be expected. Guthlac
B's combination of lamentation for the transitory
nature of all that is good and beautiful in
earthly life and rejoicing in the promises of
Heaven resembles the Libri Septem's emphasis that
man's only hope lies in God because the beauty of
human life ends in misery and death; in contrast,
De Civitate Dei does not find the destruction of
the City of Man to be in any way lamentable.

   The Orosian pattern of Guthlac B suggests a
possible conclusion which is consonant with the
poem as a whole and not more unwarranted than
others, although it is, of course, idle to attempt
to describe a lost ending authoritatively. Guthlac
B describes how Guthlac has re-enacted the cycle
of Salvation History, both Fall and Redemption, and
how his nameless disciple is re-enacting only the
first part of the cycle although he lives in the
era of Redemption, and it ends by describing an
ordinary, non-saintly person and his need for
salvation. I submit, therefore, that the ending
may have focused the audience's attention on the
need for every person to re-enact not only the Fall
of Adam but also the Redemption of Christ in his
own life and to view the history of the human race
in himself as well as in Adam, Guthlac, and the
disciple. Such an ending would be consonant with
the didactic purpose of hagiographic literature,
which seeks to persuade its readers to emulate the
heroic virtues of the saints, and it would defi-
nitely present the Orosian view that human history
is an ever-repeated and repeatable cycle of events.
The Libri Septem ends with an exhortation to all
pagans that they "molitionum suarum paeniteat
ueritatique erubescant Deumque uerum et solum, qui
potest omnia, credant timeant diligant et sequantur"
(p. 563) [repent of their deeds and blush at the
truth and believe in, fear, love, and follow the
true and only God, Who can do all things]. Furthermore, such an ending might have been expected in an
Old English hagiographic poem, for it would resemble that of Elene, whose epilogue turns away
from the story of the Invention of the Holy Cross
to remind the members of the audience that they

need to turn to the Cross for salvation as the characters in the poem have done because "þeos world eall gewiteð" (l. 1277) [this world will completely pass away] and at its end "dryhten sylf dom geseceð / engla weorude" (ll. 1280a-81a) [the Lord Himself will approach the Judgment with a host of angels].

In brief, the foregoing discussion has argued that <u>Guthlac B</u> tells how the Fall of Man is re-enacted in the lives of all the descendants of Adam and suggests that the Redemption should be re-enacted by them as well. <u>Guthlac B</u> presents the Orosian view that human history is a cycle by expressing the ideas of the <u>Libri Septem</u> in poetic form. Furthermore, it distorts the linear dimension of history and makes events in the lives of Adam, Christ, and Guthlac seem simultaneous, and it thereby suggests that the cycles of Fall and Redemption are co-existent and constantly repeated. The poem is a self-contained cycle which progresses from the Fall at the beginning of the world through the end of the Redemptive cycle in Guthlac's life and then begins again with the Fall in the life of another person. In this cyclical and static narrative, Guthlac is not merely a type of Christ and Adam as he is in Felix's Augustinian <u>Vita Guthlaci</u>. Instead, he becomes them when he re-enacts the crucial events of their lives in his own. Thus considered, <u>Guthlac B</u> is neither disjunctive nor incoherent: it is a unified cycle to which we may compare our own lives in which we are re-enacting the Fall and in which we should also be re-enacting the Redemption. By ending with a description of a man trapped in the cycle of the Fall, <u>Guthlac B</u> serves as a grim warning about the fate of those who refuse the salvation brought by Christ, in contrast to <u>Guthlac A</u>, which ends with a description of the preternatural joy of Heaven which is the reward of the redeemed.

Section B
Saintly Death and Heroic Journey

    The studies of Lord and his followers have shown that oral poets use the elements of formulaic composition to build their poems and that, in Lord's words, "the themes lead naturally from one another to form a song which exists as a whole in the singer's mind. . . . In a traditional poem . . . there is a pull in two directions: one is toward the song being sung and the other is toward the previous uses of the same theme" (p. 94). As a result, the aesthetics of any poem using formulaic elements are affected by other uses of the same elements; Greenfield says that "the associations with other contexts using a similar formula will inevitably color a particular instance of a formula so that a whole host of overtones springs into action to support the aesthetic response."[28] Furthermore, the associations called up by the use of a formula or theme are present in the minds of the audience as well as in that of the poet. Fry has suggested that "themes prove to be a mnemonic device as much for the audience as for the poet; they provide the audience with a supply of associations, which are used by the poet to enrich the narrative"[29] and which affect the aesthetic response of the audience. Many Old English poems, however, seem to be the products of written rather than oral composition; Larry D. Benson has pointed out that "the lovely Old English Phoenix . . . [is] a translation . . . so close to its Latin source that it is almost impossible to assume that its poet worked in the traditional way of hearing a tale, meditating on it, and then simultaneously singing and composing his own version."[30] Nevertheless, because a long oral tradition lies behind all written Old English poems, the latter may well have evoked a response similar to that evoked by oral works. John Miles Foley has argued that "echoes from one occurrence of a given theme reverberate not simply throughout the subsequent linear length of the given poem, but through the collective mythic knowledge of the given culture."[31] "The collective mythic knowledge" would undoubtedly have influenced the audience's reaction to written as well as to orally-composed works.

Like Guthlac A, Guthlac B is both a work composed by a literate author and one which exhibits many of the traits of the formulaic style of heroic poetry. The extent of the poem's debt to the heroic tradition is, however, open to debate. Cherniss, who has analyzed the Germanic background of Old English religious poetry, believes that Guthlac B includes only a "few traces of heroic concepts . . . [and those] appear to be for the most part mere verbal echoes, almost entirely divorced from the complex of ideas which in heroic poetry forms a consistent view of the secular world" (p. 239). In contrast, Cornell suggests that Guthlac B does use the "complex of ideas" of heroic poetry, and she uses a statistical analysis of the formulaic half-lines of Guthlac B to show that the poem "operates more obviously within the vernacular Old English poetic tradition than does Guthlac A, borrowing a greater number of . . . heroic formulae from that tradition than did A" (p. 185).

Guthlac B describes the death of the saint in a close paraphrase of Felix's description thereof. Although the passage resembles many hagiographic death scenes, it is described in terms of one of the most common formulaic themes of Old English poetry, which David K. Crowne has called the Hero on the Beach. In his article on the subject, Crowne listed the passage describing the death of Guthlac as one of the typical examples "of the occurrence of the theme in the surviving corpus of poems."[32] Likewise, in his discussion of the "variations of the Hero on the Beach theme,"[33] Fry describes the passage in Guthlac B as part of his preface to an examination of the aesthetic relevance of the theme to Judith. In a recent article, I have re-examined the passage "from the respective points of view of both the hagiographer and the oral-formulaist" and concluded that "the death of Guthlac reveals both the use of formulaic devices

of composition to express its hagiographic message
and the fact that the theme of the Hero on the
Beach fulfills an important structural function in
the poem."[34] Its purpose is similar to that which
Fry has identified as part of the aesthetic relevance of the theme to Judith: it enables the
audience to "experience the aesthetic pleasure inherent in the fulfillment of familiar, anticipated
patterns, . . . [has] a structural function . . .
[because it allows] 'poetic elaboration,' . . .
[and contributes] to unity and continuity."[35]

Fry lists the passage as a "variant" form of
the theme because, although "there is one hero,
one beach, . . . and one dawn, . . . each of the
other thematic elements is doubled."[36] In contrast to Fry, I argue that the theme does not
merely have some thematic elements, but instead
appears twice, with two heroes and two locations
which serve as beaches. Renoir has suggested that
because "a beach is by definition the separation
between two worlds--that of the land and that of
the waters--and 'the hero on the beach' necessarily
stands at the juncture between the two,"[37] the
beach may be symbolized by any location which represents such a separation. In the first appearance of the theme, Guthlac is the hero, his servant is his retainer, and flashing lights appear
before Guthlac departs on his journey of death.
Renoir has pointed out that a doorway can represent a beach because "in a less obvious but equally real way . . . [it is] the juncture between two
worlds--that of the finite inside and that of the
infinite outside";[38] Fry has suggested that the
doorway is the equivalent of a beach in two Old
English poems, The Fight at Finnsburh and Judith.[39]
I argue that "if one accepts Renoir's point, one
may likewise find a symbolic beach in Guthlac B
insofar as the wall against which the saint leans
to die separates the 'finite inside' of his hermitage from the 'infinite outside' world."[40]

In the second appearance of the theme, Guthlac's servant is the Hero on the Beach. The
scene begins when "cwom / ofer deop gelad dægred-

woma" (ll. 1291b-92b) [the break of day came over the deep sea-path]. The light which permeates all occurrences of the theme shines brightly:

> Ða þær leoht ascan,
> beama beorhtast; eal þæt beacen wæs
> ymb þæt halge hus, heofonlic leoma
> from foldan up swylce fyren tor
> ryht arǣred oð rodera hrof,
> gesewen under swegle, sunnan beorhtra,
> æþeltungla wlite.
> (ll. 1308b-14a)

[Then a light shone there, the brightest of beams; that sign was all around that holy house, the heavenly light was raised up from the earth like a fiery tower straight to the vault of the heavens, visible under the sky, brighter than the sun, than the beauty of the noble stars.]

A group of retainers is present, not in the service of Guthlac's disciple but in that of God; the term which describes the angels who remain behind after their fellows have carried Guthlac to Heaven is "engla þreatas . . . [and] 'þreatas' implies a military accompaniment."[41] The "engla þreatas" are actually present in the hermitage, in contrast to their absence in the scene as depicted in the Vita Guthlaci, which says only that "cantantibus quoque angelis spatium totius aeris detonari audiebatur" (p. 158) [the whole air was heard to resound with the songs of angels]. The Vita not only fails to describe any angelic hosts hovering around the hermitage, but also refuses to state directly that there was any angelic singing; instead, it merely reports that songs were heard by some unspecified person and does not, in contrast to normal hagiographic practice, name the reliable witness who heard them. Guthlac B restructures the vague rumor reported by the Vita into a scene which includes the troops of retainers necessary to the presence of the theme of the Hero on the Beach. The action takes place on an actual beach, implied, as Fry points out,[42] by the word "ealond" (l. 1325b)

97

[island] and by the fact that a voyage can take place. The journey begins when the "beorn unhyðig" (l. 1328a) [unhappy man] departs and gets on board a "bat" (l. 1328b) [boat], and it provides the fourth element in the second occurrence of the theme:

>   Wæghengest wræc;   wæterþisa for
>   snel under sorgum.   Swegl hate scan
>   blac ofer burgsalo;   brimwudu scynde,
>   leoht, lade fus;   lagumearg snyrede
>   gehlæsted to hyðe   þæt se hærnflota
>   æfter sundplegan   sondlond gespearn,
>   grond wið greote.
>   (ll. 1329a-35a)

[The sea-horse drove forwards, the water-rusher moved, swift under the sorrowful one. The sky shone hot, shining over the city-halls; the sea-wood hurried, bright, eager for the journey; the sea-horse hastened burdened to the harbor, so that the sea-floater struck against the sandy shore after tossing in the waves, ground against the gravel.]

Both the *Vita* and the Old English prose version thereof emphasize that the journey is one "quo vir Dei praceperat" (p. 158) [which the man of God ordered] "to þære stowe þe se Godes wer ær bebead"[43] [to that place which the man of God formerly commanded]. *Guthlac B*, however, emphasizes instead that this is a journey which leaves one beach and ends on another, and by using five different kennings for boat, it reminds the audience of formulaic descriptions of voyages in Old English heroic poetry.

The presence of the theme of the Hero on the Beach in *Guthlac B* would not necessarily mean that it is artistically used, for one may wish to agree with Bonjour that a theme can be used "rather mechanically, and, if not exactly out of context, at least without the full force of what we might call its virtual valences or associational powers"

98

(p. 566). Janet Thormann has shown that the theme is present "in 'The Phoenix' in a form considerably changed. . . . the hero . . . is a bird, . . . the beach is suggested by the word 'yðmere,' . . . [and] the blinking light is the rising sun. . . . The modifications of the theme are explained by the religious allegory."[44] Thormann believes that "the theme integrates the descriptive and narrative with the didactic parts of the poem and thus provides a unifying structure" (p. 190), but its appearance in The Phoenix does not seem as appropriate as it is in poems like Andreas or the Hildebrandlied.[45] Rather, it seems as if the translator, inspired by Lactantius' description of the "turba . . . ovans" [rejoicing crowd of men] and the "alituum . . . choro"[46] [company of winged creatures] who admire the re-born Phoenix before his journey to Paradise, described the scene in terms of the theme of the Hero on the Beach. Crowne points out that the theme of the Hero on the Beach "frequently precedes a description of (or reference to) a scene of carnage in which the theme of the Beasts of Battle is used" (p. 372), and he cites its use in Andreas, Elene, Exodus, and Judith to prove his contention. The theme also exists before descriptions of battles in which the Beasts of Battle do not appear, as is the case in the Hildebrandlied, which describes how the warriors meet "untar herjun tuem" [between two armies] with the sunlight gleaming on their "brunnono" [coats of mail].[47] Bonjour has described the theme of the Beasts of Battle as "a visible illustration of the haunting thought that death is foreordained for every man on earth . . . Wyrd . . . looms large behind the theme" (p. 566). The theme of the Hero on the Beach, whether or not it appears in conjunction with that of the Beasts of Battle, also seems to predict ill-omened events. An appropriate use of the theme, therefore, should involve some prediction of impending battle or death, as in Judith, where it appears before the Bethulian army marches to battle or in the Hildebrandlied, where it forecasts Hadubrand's death.

I have suggested that the theme of the Hero on the Beach is used in Guthlac B with aesthetic

felicity because it reinforces the polemical
message of the poem. Its first appearance predicts
Guthlac's death, although that death has no ominous
implications because when Guthlac dies, he sends
forth his spirit "weorcum wlitigne in wuldres
dream" (l. 1304) [beautiful with good works into
the joy of Heaven]. The joy which is expressed in
this passage shows that Guthlac, the saintly hero
of the Christian era, overcomes the tragic implications of the theme of the old era just as Christ
Himself overcomes those of the theme of the Cliff
of Death in Christ II. The second occurrence of
the theme likewise has an important structural
function in Guthlac B, for it provides a transition
between the vision of Heaven and the reality of
life in a fallen world, and it prepares us for the
sorrowful end of Guthlac B.

    Because it precedes a sorrowful event, the
second occurrence of the theme of the Hero on the
Beach is closer to instances in heroic poems than
is the first. In the Hildebrandlied, for example,
the theme foreshadows the grief of a father who is
forced to slay his only son and die without an heir,
and who laments, "Nu scal mih suasat chind suertu
hauwan, / breton sinu billju, eddo ih imo ti banin
werdan" (ll. 53a-54b) [Now must the beloved young
man hew me with a sword, or else I will be his
slayer]. The second occurrence of the theme in
Guthlac B forecasts the misery of the disciple who
is bereft of his lord, and more than one-third of
the last forty-five lines of our extant poem describe his misery and his "wopes hring" (l. 1339b)
[circle of lamentation]. In contrast, the analogous
point of the Vita describes not the disciple's grief
but that of Guthlac's sister Pega: "Illa vero, his
auditis, velut in praecipitium delapsa, se solo
premens, immensi maeroris molestia medullitus
emarcuit, lingua siluit, labrum obmutuit, omnique
vivali vigore velut exanimis evanuit" (pp. 158 and
160) [Having heard these things, she truly fell in
a headlong fall, and as she lay on the ground, she
withered away inwardly from the affliction of her
immeasurable grief; her tongue was silent, her
lips became speechless, and all her life and

strength vanished, as if she were dead]. Like some other Latin hagiographic works, as, for example, Gregory the Great's description of the life of St. Benedict, the Vita emphasizes the relationship between the brother and sister, whereas Guthlac B emphasizes the heroic relationship between lord and thane.

As Guthlac B now stands, it ends with the disciple's lament that he must "sarigferð / heanmod hweorfan hyge drusendne" (ll. 1378b-79b) [depart sorrowing in soul, dejected in spirit, with a drooping mind]. Although the lament is incomplete, the sorrow expressed in it is such that the emotional undercurrent generated by the Hero on the Beach passage is completed and recalls to us the many ominous situations in which the theme occurs. Charles William Kennedy compares the spirit of this passage to "the elegiac strains of the Wanderer,"[48] and Greenfield states that "the lord-thane relationship--at heart a Germanic concept--is developed gradually as the poem proceeds, culminating in the end . . . as the servant flees to his ship to seek the saint's sister and reports to her in exile-elegiac fashion."[49] Cornell comments that the disciple "utters laments of deprivation and exile characteristic of the typical worldly thane of heroic tradition" (p. 182), and, in our extant text, Guthlac B ends with a vision of the darkness of exile and the hopelessness of fallen man.

Section C
Guthlac B: The Composite View

As we have seen, Guthlac B is not a joyous poem as Guthlac A is, partly because it does not end with a description of the joys of Heaven. In addition, it presents the Orosian view that human history is a cycle in which sorrow always follows joy and in which each person inevitably re-enacts Adam's Fall but may choose to re-enact Christ's Redemption. The poem ends with a description of the sorrow of Guthlac's disciple, who has been trapped in the cycle of the Fall. Some critics maintain that a long passage is missing from the end of Guthlac B; Langen, for example, states that "it does not seem possible that the poem was meant to end with the pronouncements of Beccel; the misery in them needs to be resolved" (p. 101). The misery does not, however, necessarily call for resolution on either theological or literary grounds. Orosius' seven books are full of the stories of people who came to miserable ends, and the only thing which separates Christian times from pre-Christian is "praesentem magis Christi gratiam" (p. 564) [the greater presence of Christ's grace], which prevents the Goths from destroying Rome completely but does not really improve the human situation. When we consider Guthlac B from an oral-formulaic point of view, we realize that its misery "does not necessarily call for resolution because the theme of the Hero on the Beach inevitably precedes a hopeless situation. . . . Thus, both the theological work whose ideas underlie Guthlac B and the formulaic theme at the end of our extant text lead us to expect that the conclusion of the poem might well have been as gloomy as the present ending."[50] The Guthlac B poet uses his inherited Germanic poetic language and images to express his Christian purpose, for he uses the theme of the Hero on the Beach twice to parallel his Orosian concepts. Guthlac, at the end of the cycle of the Redemption, escapes from what is always a hopeless situation when it occurs in heroic poetry, but his disciple, caught in the middle of the cycle of the Fall, is overcome by the full misery predicted by the theme.

The theme of the Hero on the Beach is used appropriately in Guthlac B, and it serves the same purposes which Fry believes that it serves in Judith: it allows the audience to observe the fulfillment of familiar patterns, it is part of the structure of the poem, and it contributes to the

unity and coherence of the poem, in the case of
Guthlac B by emphasizing the theological message.
The theme is used appropriately in Guthlac B because
its details are neither merely poetic elaboration
nor what Crowne calls "elements of the traditional
theme which the poet is using to fill in this part
of the plan of the story" (p. 367). Fry suggests
that it is largely irrelevant to Guthlac B when
he states that "without its flashing light, the
Hero on the Beach theme ceases to exist, yet the
light is seldom essential to the plot . . . the
gleam of Heaven and the shining sky in Guthlac
1289b-1332a [are superfluous]; but the traditional
form and content of the theme required all these
lights."[51] The lights are not, however, merely
poetic elaboration of a story used to fulfill a
traditional theme, for they are found in the
analogous passage in the Vita, and the lights which
shine during the night of Guthlac's death are of
crucial thematic importance both in the Vita and
in Guthlac B because they help demonstrate Guthlac's
sanctity. Bertram Colgrave shows that the Vita's
description of Guthlac's death is replete with
such thematic details, for in addition to the
shining heavenly light, he notes as common hagiographic proofs of sanctity "Guthlac's foreknowledge
of his death, . . . [the fact that he forbids]
those who had witnessed a miracle to make any mention of it until after his death, . . . [and] the
sweet odour associated with . . . [his] death."[52]
As a result, without the shining light, the
original audience of the poem might have failed
to perceive both the sanctity of Guthlac and the
presence of the theme of the Hero on the Beach.

In view of these observations, I submit that
Guthlac B is an effective poem which uses a static
and cyclical narrative form to explore the way in
which the history of the Fall and Redemption of
mankind is re-enacted in the lives of human beings,
as typified by Guthlac. It expresses its didactic
message in the traditional, formulaic language of
Old English poetry, choosing from the formulas and
themes those which most appropriately convey the
spirit and purpose of its Orosian message and

using the theme of the Hero on the Beach in a way that is unique in our surviving corpus of poetry.

Notes to Chapter Three

[1] Calder, "Theme and Strategy," p. 227.

[2] Greenfield, *Critical History*, pp. 123 and 121.

[3] James L. Rosier, "Death and Transfiguration: Guthlac B," *Philological Essays in Old and Middle English Literature and Language in Honor of Herbert Dean Merritt*, ed. James L. Rosier (Paris: Mouton, 1970), p. 82. All further references appear in the text.

[4] Benjamin P. Kurtz, "From St. Anthony to St. Guthlac: A Study in Biography," *Univ. of California Publications in Modern Philology*, 12 (1926), p. 143. All further references appear in the text.

[5] Calder, "Theme and Strategy," p. 228.

[6] Lord implies that the beginnings of poems are their most stable parts when he says, "One of the reasons also why different singings of the same song by the same man vary most in their endings is that the end of the song is sung less often by the singer" [*The Singer of Tales*, p. 17].

[7] Calder, "*Guthlac A* and *Guthlac B*," p. 69.

[8] Greenfield, *Critical History*, p. 121.

[9] Calder, "Theme and Strategy," p. 228.

[10] Geoffrey Chaucer, *The Works of Geoffrey Chaucer*, ed. F. N. Robinson, 2nd. ed. (Boston: Houghton Mifflin Co., 1961), p. 84.

[11] Olsen, "Guthlac on the Beach," *Neophilologus*, 64 (1980), p. 290. Some of the ideas expressed in this chapter expand points suggested in the article. In "De Historiis Sanctorum," I have argued briefly that Orosius influenced many hagiographers.

¹²Paulus Orosius, <u>Historiarum Adversum Paganos Libri Septem, Accedit Eiusdem Liber Apologeticus</u>, ed. Carolus Zangemeister, Corpus Scriptorum Ecclesiasticorum Latinorum, vol. 5 (Vindobonae: C. Geroldi Filium Bibliopolam Academiae, 1882), p. 7. All further references appear in the text. All translations are mine.

¹³Calder, "Theme and Strategy," p. 233.

¹⁴In "The Uses of Irony," Black argues both that <u>Guthlac A</u> and <u>B</u> depict the devils in a fashion derived from Athanasius and Prudentius and that <u>Guthlac B</u> is a <u>psychomachia</u>; I am arguing the opposite point: that the devils are real.

¹⁵Hanning, <u>Vision of History</u>, p. 36.

¹⁶Calder, "Theme and Strategy," p. 236.

¹⁷See, for example, Ælfric, <u>The Homilies of the Anglo-Saxon Church</u>, ed. and trans. Benjamin Thorpe, vol. 1 (London: The Ælfric Society, 1844), p. 166. The Old English version of the Gospel of Matthew says that Mary is with child "of tham Halgan Gaste" [by the Holy Spirit] [<u>Tha Halgan Godspel on Englisc: The Anglo-Saxon Version of the Holy Gospels</u>, ed. Benjamin Thorpe, 2nd. ed. (New York: George P. Putnam, 1848), p. 2].

¹⁸Ælfric, <u>Homilies of the Anglo-Saxon Church</u>, vol. 1, p. 472.

¹⁹See Langen, "Commentary," pp. 90ff.

²⁰Gaspar Lefebvre, O. S. B., ed., <u>Daily Missal</u> (St. Paul, Minnesota: E. M. Lohmann Co., 1925), p. 31.

²¹Calder, "Theme and Strategy," p. 235.

²²Ælfric, <u>Homilies of the Anglo-Saxon Church</u>, vol. 2, p. 580.

²³Calder, "Theme and Strategy," p. 241.

[24] R. T. Farrell, "Some Remarks on the Exeter Book 'Azarias'," ME, 41 (1972), p. 5.

[25] Roberts, "Guðlac A, B, and C?" ME, 42 (1973), pp. 44-45.

[26] See, for example, Chambers, Förster, and Flower, eds., The Exeter Book, p. 58. Early scholars, who argued that Cynewulf was the author of Guthlac B, theorized that the lost ending contained a runic-signature passage similar to that at the end of Juliana [see, for example, Richard P. Wülcker, "Über den Dichter Cynewulf," Anglia, 1 (1878), pp. 483-507]. In The Guthlac Poems, Roberts assumes that "a gathering (or more) has dropped out of the manuscript between folios 52 and 53" (p. 43) and that "the final scope of Guthlac B cannot be gauged" (p. 48).

[27] Krapp and Dobbie, The Exeter Book, p. lxiii.

[28] Greenfield, "The Formulaic Expression of the Theme of 'Exile'," p. 205.

[29] Fry, "Heroine on the Beach," p. 181.

[30] Larry D. Benson, "The Literary Character of Anglo-Saxon Formulaic Poetry," PMLA, 81 (1966), p. 335.

[31] John Miles Foley, "Formula and Theme in Old English Poetry," Oral Literature and the Formula, ed. Benjamin A. Stolz and Richard S. Shannon, III (Ann Arbor: Center for the Coördination of Ancient and Modern Studies, 1976), p. 231.

[32] David K. Crowne, "The Hero on the Beach: An Example of Composition by Theme in Anglo-Saxon Poetry," NM, 61 (1960), p. 371. All further references appear in the text.

[33] Fry, "Heroine on the Beach," p. 177.

[34] Olsen, "Guthlac on the Beach," p. 292.

³⁵Fry, "Heroine on the Beach," pp. 182-83.

³⁶Fry, "Heroine on the Beach, p. 173.

³⁷Renoir, "Oral-Formulaic Theme Survival," p. 73.

³⁸Renoir, "Oral-Formulaic Theme Survival," p. 73.

³⁹Fry, "Heroine on the Beach," p. 173.

⁴⁰Olsen, "Guthlac on the Beach," p. 293.

⁴¹Fry, "Heroine on the Beach," p. 173.

⁴²Fry, "Heroine on the Beach," p. 173.

⁴³Goodwin, ed., The Anglo-Saxon Version of the Life of St. Guthlac, p. 88.

⁴⁴Janet Thormann, "Variations on the Theme of the 'Hero on the Beach' in 'The Phoenix'," NM, 71 (1970), pp. 188-89. All further references appear in the text.

⁴⁵Like Guthlac B, the Hildebrandlied has often been considered a fragment. In "The Kassel Manuscript and the Conclusion of the Hildebrandslied" [Manuscripta, 23 (1979), p. 107], Renoir points out that calling the extant text of the Hildebrandlied a fragment because it does not describe the death of Hadubrand "illustrates the same kind of reasoning as would lead to labelling the transmitted text of the Iliad a fragment because it fails to account for the death of Achilles. . . . Whenever a poem entirely or partly composed in accordance with the techniques of the oral-formulaic tradition seems to succeed in telling what it was presumably intended to tell and does so in a manner illustrative of the relevant requirements of that tradition, the chances are that it should be considered a relatively self-contained unit." I would argue that a similar point can be made in respect to Guthlac B.

[46] Lactantius, "Carmen de Ave Phoenice," in Blake, ed., The Phoenix, p. 91, lines 152 and 155.

[47] Hildebrandlied, ed. and trans. Gotthold Bötticher, in Hildebrandlied und Waltharilied nebst den "Zauberspruchen" und "Muspilli," Dentmäler der Älteren Deutschen Literatur, ed. Gotthold Bötticher and Karl Kinzel, vol. 1 (Halle: Verlag der Buchhandlung des Waisenhauses, 1905), pp. 4 and 8, ll. 3 and 62. All further references appear in the text.

[48] Charles William Kennedy, The Earliest English Poetry (New York and London: Oxford Univ. Press, 1943), p. 258.

[49] Greenfield, Critical History, p. 122.

[50] Olsen, "Guthlac on the Beach," p. 294.

[51] Fry, "Heroine on the Beach," p. 182.

[52] Felix, Life of Saint Guthlac, pp. 192-93.

Chapter Four
Guthlac:
A Proposed Reading of the Composite Poem

Section A
Epic and Hagiography: Medieval Unity

Hitherto, this study has followed standard modern practice and considered Guthlac A and B to be separate works.[1] Roberts has applied "the criteria put forward by A. J. Bliss . . . in 'The Metre of "Beowulf"'"[2] to Guthlac; after an examination of contractions, finite verbs, alliteration, and hypermetric verses, she has concluded that Guthlac A and B "are by poets different both in identity and period. Guthlac A resembles most of all the earlier Anglo-Saxon poems. . . . By comparison with the second Guthlac poem, Guthlac A is plain. It has no passages of extended simile and nothing comparable with the B-poet's development of the figure of death. . . . [Its] kennings are less striking, for they are generally descriptive and rarely metaphorical."[3] Although from the point of view of linguistics and metrics I am in complete agreement with Roberts' contention that there were originally two poems, I should like to suggest that it is nevertheless possible to read the text of Guthlac as it appears in the Exeter Book as a single poem.

The manuscript gives no indication that Anglo-Saxon readers would necessarily have considered Guthlac A and B to be separate works; in fact, as Margaret E. Goldsmith has pointed out, it suggests that the poems were "designed to be read as a sequence."[4] The scribe of the Exeter Book has indicated the beginning of each poem and the major sections thereof by large initial capital letters. In nine places, however, an entire line is capitalized: the beginnings of six poems, including Guthlac, and lines 440 and 867 of Christ and 879 of Guthlac. Most critics believe that the divisions in Christ and Guthlac indicate the beginnings of new poems, yet one may plausibly argue that the scribe intended them to indicate new sections rather than new poems. In fact, modern editors tacitly acknowledge the ambiguity of the evidence by numbering the lines of Guthlac A and B consecutively rather than separately.[5] Medieval authors often wrote conclusions for incomplete works and intended the composites to be read as unified wholes. For example, even though Jean de Meung's continuation of the Roman de la Rose differs substantially from the original by Guillaume de Lorris, it begins with a continuation of a speech by the Lover, and modern scholars talk of a single Roman as well as of the separate sections.

I have no desire, therefore, to dismiss lightly what Calder describes as "that medieval perspective which can see Guthlac A and B as one 'composite' poem,"[6] especially since the poems appear to be the written descendants of oral-formulaic songs. Robert Scholes and Robert Kellogg have emphasized the fact that "the singer . . . neither composes nor memorizes a fixed text. Each performance is a separate act of creation."[7] As a result, the works a singer composes "are manifestations of a tradition rather than the inventions of an individual brain . . . and the bookish attitudes toward authorship which come so naturally to literate men . . . must be quite incomprehensible to oral poets" (p. 22). Even the poems of Cynewulf, whose runic signatures suggest written rather than oral composition, "were composed out of the common Anglo-Saxon oral tradition and cannot represent the work of an individual poet in anything like the modern sense" (p. 22). The compiler of Guthlac was, like Cynewulf, working in the tradition of formulaic poetry. I should like to suggest, therefore, that he may also have conceived of his work as a manifestation of that tradition and that--to borrow the statement about the author of Sæmundar Edda made by Scholes and Kellogg--"we should conceive of his role as singer or performer as coming closer than the modern concept of 'authorship' to describing the man behind the poem" (p. 23).

I submit that we are not taking unwarranted
liberties when we read <u>Guthlac</u>, a work presumably
of multiple authorship, as a single, unified poem,
nor are we necessarily adopting a "medieval perspective" by so doing. Numerous literary works,
considered to be units by modern readers, were
composed by more than one author, among which the
most celebrated are Goldsmith's "The Traveler"
and "The Deserted Village." Samuel Johnson con-
tributed lines to both poems, but they are, nevertheless, unified works. Even Johnson could not be
entirely certain how many lines he wrote for "The
Traveler," for, although he "told Reynolds that
'the utmost that I have wrote in that poem, to the
best of my recollections, is not more than eighteen
lines' . . ., in 1783 when he marked his contribu-
tion for Boswell, nine lines were all of which he
could be sure."[8] I believe that it is valuable to
read <u>Guthlac</u> as its compiler and original audience
may well have done: as a single hagiographic poem
about St. Guthlac of Croyland. Because of the
nature of the <u>Exeter Book</u>, we do not have <u>Guthlac
A</u> and <u>Guthlac B</u> as they were originally composed.
Scholars agree that "the stately, even style of
the writing . . . [shows] that the scribe of the
Exeter Book was copying from an anthology which
was already in existence [and that,] because the
codex shows a surprising comformity in language,
it must have been copied by a succession of scribes
who were not only able, but also regarded themselves
as free to standardize the spelling of the manuscript they were copying."[9]

It is possible that scribes who felt free to
standardize spelling may also have felt free to
combine the texts they were copying into a form
possibly different from their originals. As a
result, our only extant text reflects, not the in-
tentions of the authors of <u>Guthlac</u> <u>A</u> and <u>B</u>, but
rather those of the person who combined the two
poems at some point after their composition. As
<u>Guthlac</u> <u>B</u> appears in the manuscript, for example,
it tempts us to believe that it was composed in
writing, for it appeals to written rather than
oral tradition and says that "us secgað bec"

(1. 878b) [books tell us] about Guthlac. Furthermore, __Guthlac B__ lacks the traditional epic beginning which characterizes both heroic and hagiographic poetry, for it begins in an almost conversational way which would undoubtedly fail to catch the attention of an audience listening to an oral composition:

> Ðæt is wide cuð wera cneorissum,
> folcum gefræge, þætte frymþa God
> þone ærestan   ælda cynnes
> of þære clænestan, cyning ælmihtig,
> foldan geworhte.
> (ll. 819a-23a)

> [It is widely known to the generations of men, well-known to the peoples, that the God of beginnings, the Almighty King, made the first of the race of men from the purest earth.]

It is, however, impossible to decide whether the beginning of our extant __Guthlac B__ is the original beginning of the original poem. The compiler may have deleted an attention-getting "Hwæt!" or a similar formula in order to make the poem follow __Guthlac A__ smoothly and to make its tone similar to that of __Guthlac A__, which also begins in a non-dramatic fashion: "Se bið gefeana fægrast þonne hy æt frymðe gemetað, / engel 7 seo eadge sawl" (ll. 1a-2a) [That is the fairest of joys when they first meet, the angel and the blessed soul]. I should like to propose a reading which will both argue the unity of our only extant text of __Guthlac__ and suggest why the poems were placed successively in a way which still tempts us to read them as one, as it presumably did the audience for whom the __Exeter Book__ was originally intended. In the following discussion, I shall refer to __Guthlac__'s two sections as __Guthlac A__ and __B__ in order to use consistent terminology throughout the study.

Since I have suggested that __Guthlac__ may profitably be read as a composite poem, I should like to mention the analogous case of Old French and Old Norse works which are composites but which are read as unified works.[10] One Old French poem that shows greater structural disparities than does Guthlac is Raoul de Cambrai, a late twelfth-century chanson de geste composed of 344 laisses, of which the first 249 are in rhyme and the last 95 in assonance. The difference between these two metrical forms is far more significant than are the variations in the Old English alliterative line found in Guthlac A and Guthlac B.[11] Raoul de Cambrai's two sections also exhibit major thematic differences, for the rhymed portion deals exclusively with the epic theme of the conflict between a man's loyalties to his kindred and his lord;[12] in contrast, the assonant portion deals with the themes of love and sorcery, which are more commonly found in the courtly romances. The titular hero of the poem, Raoul, is slain in laisse 183, and although the remainder of the rhymed portion describes the war which follows his death, the assonant section describes the love affair of Raoul's slayer, Bernier. The two sections are linked only the fact that Raoul's murder is avenged at the end of the poem, and since they exhibit major discrepancies in plot, style, and language, they are likewise more strikingly different from each other than are the sections of Guthlac, which show continuity of hero and subject; in fact, Raoul de Cambrai seems to be a composite of two other chansons de geste, one about Raoul de Cambrai and one about Bernier.

Critics of Old English poetry assume that Guthlac cannot be read as a single poem because, despite the "medieval editor's rough attempt at a biographical unity,"[13] the second section repeats events described in the first, the most important of which is Guthlac's death. Roberts maintains that since "Guthlac actually dies in both these poems . . . the presentation of the case for a single Guthlac poem . . . suggests a misreading of Guthlac A."[14] Old French chansons de geste show similar discrepancies, however, especially in the case of La Chanson de Guillaume, which is probably a composite, because two other chansons de geste, Chevalerie Vivien and Aliscans, recount the stories found in its first and second sections. Unlike Raoul de Cambrai, La Chanson de Guillaume has a single subject and hero, but the two sections contradict each other on several important thematic points. In its first section, the poem describes the death of Guillaume's nephew Vivien in a battle against the Saracen king Desramed and then states that Guillaume avenges him by slaying Desramed and routing the Saracen army. A few lines thereafter, however, at the beginning of the second section, Guillaume finds Vivien on the battlefield, mortally wounded, and the two talk together before Vivien dies. Guillaume's army is routed by Desramed, and the poem continues for an additional 1,514 lines before Desramed is slain and Guillaume wins the battle for the second--and final--time. Many scholars believe that the stories represented by Chevalerie Vivien and Aliscans were combined into a single chanson de geste,[15] and I submit that we are as justified in reading Guthlac as a composite as in reading La Chanson de Guillaume as one, for although both show continuity of subject and hero, the miraculous resurrection of Vivien is more surprising than the fact that Guthlac's death is described twice in one poem.[16] Since Guthlac, Raoul de Cambrai, and La Chanson de Guillaume are each found in a single manuscript, critical theories cannot be supported by the evidence of other manuscripts and are, therefore, unprovable.

Some Old Norse sagas exhibit less narrative unity than do the chansons de geste, yet they are demonstrably works written by a single author. Often a work which derives its title from a hero whose adventures it recounts at length is nevertheless a composite. Grettis Saga, for example, is primarily an episodic work describing the battles of Grettir against men and monsters. In addition, however, it recounts the stories of Grettir's great-grandfather Onundr, grandfather Thorgrim, and father Asmundr, and its conclusion, which describes how Grettir's half-brother Thorstein avenges Grettir's death, is an adaptation of the

story of Tristan and Isolde. Mason has commented
that the prose Vǫlsunga Saga is "based on older
poetry, some of which has been lost. In particular,
those chapters which concern Sigurðr's youth and
his slaying of Fáfnir are heavily dependent on the
poems which are known, in their present fragmentary
state, as the Reginsmál and Fáfnismál" (p. 219).
Mason concludes that "as a composite work, the
Vǫlsunga Saga is sometimes confusing, and it is
often inferior to those poems still extant on
which it is based. However, it tries with considerable success to present a reasonable family history
for the most celebrated monster-slayer of Germanic
Antiquity" (p. 227). The author of the Vǫlsunga
Saga seems to have been motivated by reasons similar
to those that I argue may have been held by the
compiler of Guthlac: to restructure disparate works
into a single story about a heroic figure.

Many modern critics consider that works like
those discussed above lack unity, and modern ideas
about narrative unity may be exemplified by William
C. Calin's description thereof: "If a poem is
coherent as to narrative, theme, style, and atmosphere--if every major episode contributes to the
whole and, if left out, would leave an important
gap; if the major themes permeate the entire work
without clashing; if the atmosphere or atmospheres
and style are consistent and in harmony with
characters and plot--then (given an adequate manuscript) the text can be considered authentic and
valid, and the poem a unified whole. It may well
be that this sense of structure and organic unity
is the only way of determining a work of art."[17]
This conception of narrative unity may be profitably applied to many literary works, but the value
of its application to chansons de geste, Old English
poetry, and hagiography is questionable. In the
case of the chansons de geste, for example, which
J. Rychner has argued were not merely written for
oral delivery but were actually orally composed,[18]
such a kind of unity is extremely unlikely. As
even Calin has noted, the extant chansons de geste
"were practically always the work of more than one
poet" (p. 13), but, like the Roman de la Rose, they

were intended to be read as units. In addition, "most specialists feel that the extant chansons de geste were based on oral tradition but reworked by clerks who set them down in writing";[19] the extant chansons are, therefore, like Guthlac, scribal compilations of several already-existing works. We should hesitate to apply modern standards of unity to works which are the joint products of oral and written composition, and it is reasonable to assume that the second poet or the scribe who combined two works into a third one did so for reasons which seemed to him logical. We should especially be willing to make such an assumption when works exhibit not "organic unity" but another, although equally logical, coherence. As the foregoing study has argued, each of the individual Guthlac poems is coherent, although various modern critics have considered either or both of them disorganized. I would argue that Guthlac also exhibits coherence and should be considered a unified work.

Modern critics have also attempted to impose their ideas about narrative unity upon hagiographic works, which, like the sagas and the chansons de geste, are based on a mixture of oral and written traditions. Hippolyte Delehaye believes that, as a result of the many intermediaries between an event and the final literary work in which it is described, stories naturally become confused with each other: "Il arrive à l'homme le plus véridique et le plus intègre de créer, sans s'en apercevoir, de petites légendes en introduisant dans ses récits ses impressions, ses raisonnements, ses passions, et de ne présenter la vérité qu'embellie ou défigurée, selon les circonstances. Ces sources d'erreurs . . . se multiplient avec le nombre des intermédiaires."[20] Furthermore, hagiographers borrowed themes, incidents, and even passages from other works, and many of the most interesting hagiographic narratives violate several of Calin's dicta about the nature of narrative unity and literary artistry. The fact that hagiographic works contain passages borrowed from earlier works about different saints has tempted some modern critics to suggest that all examples are identical, regardless of date, place of composition, or authorial intention; James Whitby Earl, for example, maintains that "when you've read one saint's life, you've read them all."[21] Hagiographic works tend to be conventional because they were composed for liturgical use; therefore, as Jones has pointed out, "originality might make the work more palatable, but it was not the end or aim. And after the audience had heard the story [of St. Cuthbert] read, each year again come Cuthbert's Day, originality would lose its point" (p. 73). Most hagiographic works also contain episodes which could be deleted without changing either the purpose or the atmosphere of the works, but which emphasize the didactic messages thereof. Even Athansius' Vita Sancti Antonii--which many critics feel is the model for medieval hagiographic works--contains numerous passages which repeat previous ones in order to emphasize didactic points. Felix's Vita itself exemplifies the fact that hagiographic works tend to be composites, for its preface is, as Jones says, "a florilegium of word-for-word quotations" (p. 54) from earlier works, and Felix has borrowed incidents and quotations freely to use in the remainder of the Vita.

Medieval hagiographers felt free either to summarize or to expand the material in an earlier work. Ordericus Vitalis, for example, made "a revision of the life of St. Guthlac . . . [known as the] Abbrevatio,"[22] and William of Malmesbury expanded earlier hagiographic works about St. Swithin, which consisted primarily of descriptions of his posthumous miracles, to include a life-story appropriate for a saintly bishop. The fact that hagiographers felt free to revise and adapt the works of other authors, summarizing or incorporating borrowed passages whenever they wished, suggests that hagiographic works were not considered unified and unchangeable in the same way as modern narratives are. In fact, the narrative unity which individual hagiographic works have is not represented by "structure and organic unity" as twentieth-century critics expect. Furthermore, hagiographic works seldom attempt to depict fully-drawn personages. Sometimes hagiographers delete information which would detract from the saintly picture, as Ælfric deletes biographical information about King Oswald in order to present him as a great ascetic saint. In addition, all episodes and stories about miracles are equally relevant to a work like Felix's _Vita_, which seems to be "pious propaganda"[23] intended to make the cult of St. Guthlac as important as that of St. Cuthbert. Felix has borrowed from many Latin works, including "the Life of St. Cuthbert . . . some of the works of Aldhelm . . . Sulpicius Severus's _Vita Martini_ . . . Jerome's _Vita Pauli_, Athanasius's _Vita Antonii_ . . . Gregory the Great's Life of St. Benedict . . . [and] Virgil."[24] Felix's own style, which tends to be, in the words of Ordericus Vitalis, "prolixus et aliquantulum obscurus"[25] [prolix and somewhat obscure], differs substantially from those of his borrowings, so that the _Vita_ is indeed what Jones has called "a florilegium" (p. 54), a patchwork of Felix's highly elaborate prose and passages borrowed from other authors. It is, however, a coherent work which evidences definite authorial intention, although it violates Calin's _dictum_ that a unified work must have a consistent style as well as harmonious characters and plot. Hagiographic narratives are concerned to express spiritual ideals, and the authors show little interest in what Calin calls coherence "as to narrative, theme, style, and atmosphere" (p. 13). Although we can only speculate because _Guthlac A_ and _B_ have not survived as individual works, the compiler of _Guthlac_ may have been like hagiographers and the scribes who copied manuscripts, because, as Gerard J. Brault says, "clerks routinely introduced many changes whenever copying except, of course, when transcribing sacred or canonical works" (p. 193). If we read hagiographic narratives with an understanding of their nature and conventions and without expecting them to resemble coherent modern biographies, we should perhaps be willing to read _Guthlac_ as a composite poem.

It is intriguing to speculate about the reasons that induced a scribe to combine two poems

into a single whole as did the compilers of La
Chanson de Guillaume and Guthlac. In the case of
Guthlac, one may speculate that the reasons re-
sembled those which inspired Christians during
the Second Century to write apocryphal gospels
and acts of the apostles. Edgar J. Goodspeed has
pointed out that people tend to be curious about
the lives of those whom they venerate and that
"the Four Gospels seemed to their early readers to
leave gaps in the life of Jesus which might be
edifyingly filled, and so pointed toward further
gospel writing, [and] the Book of Acts left a mass
of loose ends that invited literary effort. . . .
In the absence of authentic memories, imagination
took the lead, and a group of religious novels
resulted."[26] Although Guthlac does not present a
complete biography of Guthlac as Felix's Vita does,
it has what Calder labels a "rough . . . biographical unity,"[27] in contrast to Guthlac A and B, each
of which seems to leave "a mass of loose ends."
The compiler might very well have wished to combine
the two partially biographical poems in order to
satisfy the literary expectations of an audience
accustomed to such works as Felix's Vita Sancti
Guthlaci, Bede's Vita Sancti Cuthberti, and Eddius'
Vita Sancti Wilfrithi Episcopi. If we compare
Guthlac A and B separately to the three other
extant Old English hagiographic poems, we find that
Elene, Juliana, and Andreas are much closer to
their respective sources than are the two Guthlac
poems and that they also provide fairly full biographical information. Elene, the story of the
Invention of the Holy Cross, follows its Latin
source, the Vita Cyriaci, closely, and deletes
little biographical information about Constantine,
Elene, or Judas-Cyriacus. Juliana provides as much
information about the life and martyrdom of the
virgin martyr as is found in the annals of the
Church. Andreas is based on one of the most famous
of the apocryphal legends, that of St. Andrew's
mission to Mermedonia, and tends to add rather than
delete material. Thus, although none of the three
poems is a complete biography, each is more biographical than either Guthlac A or B and, in addition, follows its source with much greater fidelity

than the latter do. The two poems may well have been combined partly to satisfy the curiosity of the audience about the life of St. Guthlac and partly to restructure two idiosyncratic poems into a single work somewhat closer to the Latin source. The compiler would undoubtedly have been especially interested in combining the two poems if Guthlac B came to him in the fragmentary state in which it presently exists, because, in comparison to Guthlac B, Guthlac seems complete.

    Guthlac says that a saintly person must be able both to live a holy life and to die a holy death; as a result, it provides a fuller picture of Christian virtue than does Guthlac A, which defines sanctity as the ability to endure diabolic temptations, or Guthlac B, which defines it as the ability to die with fortitude. The tone and spirit of Guthlac resemble those of certain Patristic Passiones, which are seldom full biographies and are often bipartite in structure, describing in the first part how a Christian must live a holy life and in the second how he should face all torments and temptations with fortitude and die valiantly. In many ways, Guthlac resembles the earliest Christian hagiographic work, the Vita et Passio Sancti Cæcilii Cypriani, written by Pontius in 259 A.D. Pontius deliberately omits any discussion of Cyprian's pagan youth but begins his work "a principio fidei, et navitate cœlesti"[28] [from the beginning of his faith, and from his heavenly birth]. He then describes Cyprian's exemplary life as a bishop and the saint's martyrdom, for Cyprian "et sine martyrio habuit quæ doceret" (col. 1541) [even without his martyrdom had things to teach], and by his death he "etiam ad perfectam coronam, Domino conssummante profecit" (col. 1558) [gained even the perfect crown, brought to perfection by the Lord]. Although Guthlac does not narrate the passion of a martyr, it describes the life of a holy hermit, and as the Vita Cypriani points out, "semper Deo mancipata devotio, dicatis hominibus pro martyrio deputetur" (cols. 1557-58) [devotion given to God is always counted as martyrdom by consecrated men]. Guthlac might easily be

entitled <u>Vita et Passio Sancti Guthlaci</u>,[29] because
its sections provide precisely the same balance of
a heroic life and death as do those of the <u>Vita
Cypriani</u>. Like the <u>Vita Cypriani</u>, <u>Guthlac</u> displays
little interest in the fact that "se halga wer /
in þa ærestan ældu gelufade / frecnessa fela" (ll.
108b-10a) [the holy man in his first youth loved
many dangerous things] but concentrates instead on
the fact that he "in Godes willan / mod gerehte,
man eall forseah" (ll. 95b-96b) [governed his mind
according to the will of God and rejected all evil]
before dying a holy death. The poem may, therefore,
be considered a didactic work which is much closer
to examples of Graeco-Latin hagiography than are
<u>Guthlac</u> <u>A</u> and <u>B</u>.

Section B
The Re-Sung Song

     Oral-formulaists have demonstrated that poems
composed orally have no fixed texts; in the words
of Scholes and Kellogg, "we can speak of the elements of the song--the plot, the episodes, the
conception of character, the knowledge of historical
events, the traditional motifs, the diction--as
being transmitted, but we cannot speak of the oral
transmission of the song itself" (p. 23). Likewise,
if, as Brault has suggested, monastic scribes
"routinely introduced many changes whenever copying"
(p. 193), then we may assume that even written works
did not have fixed texts. I suspect that the scribe
who compiled <u>Guthlac</u> may have been familiar with
both the traditional transmission of oral-formulaic
songs and the habits of the scriptorium. As a
result, I should like to argue that he might well
have felt free to re-combine poems which came to
him from both oral and written sources. <u>Guthlac</u>
is as coherent and unified as other extant Old
English poems.

Like Beowulf or Christ and Satan, Guthlac distorts the linear dimension of time so that the audience perceives the events of the poem from a point outside the temporal sphere. Because Guthlac B gives a brief recapitulation of the temptations of the devils which A describes at length, Guthlac therefore emphasizes that human life is never free from evil and sin and that even the holiest of men faces constant temptation which he must resist "stronglice" (l. 903a) [firmly] and "geþyldum" (l. 914b) [patiently]. Guthlac A emphasizes that Guthlac is tempted repeatedly and that the temptations grow more severe as he becomes more holy, and Guthlac B re-introduces the theme of temptation even after the conclusion of Guthlac A describes Guthlac's apotheosis. Guthlac A never actually describes Guthlac's death, and when Guthlac B adds its description thereof to the description of Guthlac's triumphant apotheosis, the linear sense of life as a progression from birth to death to eternal reward or punishment is eliminated. Indeed, Guthlac makes Guthlac's life, apotheosis, and death seem to be contemporaneous events, and thus impels us to view time from a non-worldly perspective. Guthlac's description of Guthlac's earthly and eternal lives before that of his death emphasizes the importance of his life and the value of his victory and shows that the laments of his disciple are foolish because the saint's soul has gone "gegnunga to Hierusalem" (l. 813) [directly to Jerusalem] and only his body lies "belifd under lyfte" (l. 1308a) [deprived of life under the sky]. In contrast, Guthlac B, which does not have the other-worldly perspective of Guthlac A, has an elegiac tone which is reinforced by the disciple's laments. The point of view of Guthlac is reminiscent of that of Boethius's De Consolatione Philosophiae, which emphasizes that time is only important during earthly life.

Guthlac briefly describes the history of the world from a non-linear point of view. It begins with a discussion of the last events of history, for it alludes to the judgment that each soul faces after death and which is analogous to the Last

Judgment. When the angel meets the "eadge sawl"
(l. 2a) [blessed soul], he "abeodeð him Godes
ærende" (l. 5b) [declares God's message to him]:
"Nu þu most feran þider þu fundadest / longe 7
gelome" (ll. 6a-7a) [Now you may go where you have
long and frequently striven to go]. Just as the
twenty-nine line prologue contains themes and
images which make it an integral part of Guthlac A,
it is likewise an important part of Guthlac, whose
picture of Christian history would be incomplete
without the prologue's mention of judgment. The
description of the Creation by "frymþa God" (l.
820b) [the God of beginnings] is found in the
middle of the composite poem, after the allusion to
the Judgment. Furthermore, Guthlac describes the
effects of Christ's Advent on the world, that is,
the fact that human beings can win heavenly life,
before it describes the Fall which caused mankind
to lose eternal life. Thus, by distorting linear
time, it makes the Fall seem relatively unimportant
because it has already emphasized that salvation is
possible. In addition, it seems to echo St. Paul's
words: "Si enim unius delicto mors regnavit per
unum, multo magis abundantiam gratiae et donationis
et iustitiae accipientes in vita regnabunt per unum
Iesum Christum. . . . Sicut enim per inobedientiam
unius hominis peccatores constituti sunt multi,
ita et per unius oboeditionem iusti constituentur
multi" (Romans 5:17-19) [For, if by the offense of
one man death has reigned through that one, much
more those receiving abundance of grace, a gift,
and justice will reign in life through one Jesus
Christ. For if through the disobedience of one man
many have been made sinners, so many are made just
through the obedience of one man]. The intermingling of events from different times in history
provides a suitable background for the story of
Guthlac because it shows why it is necessary for
him to reject not only "man" (l. 96b) [evil] but
also "eorðlic æþelu" (l. 97a) [earthly nobility]
in order to go "on ecne geard" (l. 1267a) [into
the eternal dwelling-place]. Because Guthlac is
the hero of the poem, all events--past, present,
and future--are part of his life and can best be
understood in relation to him.

Despite the fragmentary condition of Guthlac B, Guthlac A and B are of approximately the same length, and the latter's account of death balances the former's account of earthly and eternal life. Guthlac A emphasizes that Guthlac lived a good Christian life and alludes to the important events of his life. The main portion of Guthlac A emphasizes that Guthlac, although a holy hermit, is tormented by "ealdfeonda nið, / searocræftum swiþ" (ll. 141b-42a) [the hostility of the ancient enemies, mighty in treacherous arts]. Guthlac A never actually describes Guthlac's death, but instead states that the saint undergoes transfiguration and exchanges his earthly life for the "betre lif" (l. 779b) [better life] of Heaven.

In contrast, Guthlac B mentions only a few of the events of Guthlac's life but emphasizes that he dies as a good Christian should, confident in God's promises:

> He on elne swa þeah
> ungeblyged bad beorhtra gehata,
> bliþe in burgum-- wæs þam bancofan
> æfter nihtglome neah geþrungen,
> breosthord onboren: wæs se bliþa gæst
> fus on forðweg.
> (ll. 940b-45a)

[Nevertheless he, undismayed, courageously awaited the radiant promises, happy in the strongholds--after nightfall, his bone-enclosure was hard pressed, his breast-hoard weakened: his joyous spirit was eager for departure.]

The themes of eremiticism and death balance each other in Guthlac: the eremitical life, which involves what St. Paul calls dying "cum Christo ab elementis huius mundi" (Colossians 2:20) [with Christ to the elements of this world], is opposed to physical death, which is a prelude to heavenly life. Thus, Guthlac B's description of Guthlac's death, which is missing from Guthlac A, provides a theological and literary balance to the ideas expressed in Guthlac A, and the balance may have tempted the compiler to combine the two poems.

The sections which comprise Guthlac describe the saintly life from different points of view: whereas Guthlac A does so from the non-worldly one of the saint, the devils who tempt him, and God and His angels, Guthlac B repeats the procedure from a worldly one. With the exception of Guthlac, the characters in Guthlac A are denizens of the spiritual realms. "Engel dryhtnes 7 se atela gæst" (l. 116) [the angel of the Lord and the dreadful spirit] fight for possession of his soul. Although the devils torment Guthlac, they cannot harm him because an angel, a "fæle freoðweard" (l. 173a) [faithful guardian of peace] protects him. The only character other than Guthlac named in Guthlac A is St. Bartholomew, called "dryhtnes ar, / halig of heofonum" (ll. 684b-85a) [the messenger of the Lord, holy from Heaven] and "ofermæcga" (l. 692b) [the man from above]. God takes part in Guthlac A, for it is He Who directs Guthlac's life, and it is "in Godes willan" (l. 95b) [according to the will of God] that Guthlac becomes a hermit. Guthlac A mentions that Guthlac had dealings with others, but it says only that he "oft þurh reorde abead / þam þe þrowera þeawas lufedon / Godes ærendu" (ll. 160b-62a) [often declared the messages of God in speech to those who loved the ways of the martyrs]. Guthlac A does not even specify that Guthlac preaches to other men, for "þam þe þrowera þeawas lufedon" is a phrase that can describe the angels, who rejoice at the victories of the Christian saints. In contrast to Guthlac A, Guthlac B has several human characters, and even though Guthlac is a hermit who lives in a remote part of England, he is visited by many people seeking miraculous cures:

> He monge oft þurh meaht Godes
> gehælde hygegeomre hefigra wita
> þe hine unsofte adle gebundne
> sarge gesohton of sidwegum
> freorigmode.
>   (ll. 884a-88a)

[Through the power of God, he often healed
many sad-minded people of grievous torments,
those who severely fettered with disease,
sorrowing sought him from the distant ways
sad in spirit.]

<u>Guthlac</u> A describes Guthlac's heavenly protector, St. Bartholomew, at great length, but <u>Guthlac</u> B does not mention Guthlac's angelic protector, the "engel ufancundne" (l. 1242a) [angel coming from above], until one-third of the poem is completed. Furthermore, the poem does not actually describe his visits, and Guthlac mentions them only because his disciple asks about Guthlac's mysterious nightly visitor and "þeodnes word, / ares uncuþes" (ll. 1216b-17a) [the speech of the lord, the unknown messenger]. In <u>Guthlac</u> A, Guthlac thinks only of God, but in <u>Guthlac</u> B, his last thought is for his sister, and immediately before his death, he speaks about her to his disciple, ordering him to take "lac to leofre" (l. 1298a) [a message to the beloved woman]. Furthermore, <u>Guthlac</u> B emphasizes the relationship between Guthlac and his disciple and Guthlac's loving concern for and patient teaching of the other, but <u>Guthlac</u> A mentions neither Guthlac's sister nor his disciple.

<u>Guthlac</u> A describes how Guthlac abandoned the life of an active warrior in order to retire to his hermitage, but his departure from life is the triumphant apotheosis of a saint, reminiscent of the bodily apotheosis of Elijah in the <u>Biblia Vulgata</u>: "Ecce currus igneus et equi ignei diviserunt utrumque; et ascendit Elias per turbinem in caelum" (Liber Regum Quartus 2:11) [Behold, a fiery chariot and fiery horses separated the two of them; and Elijah went up into Heaven in a whirlwind]. During the Middle Ages, authors emphasize the sanctity of heroes by recounting that their souls were carried to Heaven by angelic hosts. Renoir has suggested that the author of <u>La Chanson de Roland</u> uses the conclusion of his poem to show that Roland has repented of his sins and died as a good Christian should,[30] for, like Elijah or Guthlac, Roland goes straight to Heaven after his death:

> Deus tramist sun angle Cherubin,
> E[nsembl'od li] seint Michel del Peril;
> Ensembl'od els sent Gabriel i vint,
> l'anme del cunte portent en pareis.[31]

> [God sent his angel Cherubim, together with
> St. Michael of the perilous seas; they went
> together with St. Gabriel, and bore the
> soul of the count to Paradise.]

The end of Guthlac B emphasizes not the apotheosis of Guthlac but his death and its effect on another human being, his beloved disciple, who mourns his master and bears "gnornsorge" (l. 1335b) [sorrow] in his heart. Guthlac B thus emphasizes the human perspective at the expense of its supernatural counterpart which plays such an important part in Guthlac A, and the two sections balance Guthlac's supernatural and human concerns.

Guthlac B frequently uses imagery of exile and homelessness: after the Fall, Adam and Eve "scofene wurdon / on gewinworuld" (ll. 856b-57a) [were thrust into a world of care], the devils who torment Guthlac are "hiwes binotene, / dreamum bidrorene" (ll. 900b-1a) [berett of beauty, deprived of joys], Guthlac lives and dies in exile, and his disciple is left after Guthlac's death in the state of an exiled retainer mourning "dryhtenbealu" (l. 1349a) [the loss of his lord]. The imagery of exile in Guthlac B is typical of that in other Christian works, and the mood of the poem may be compared to that of Paradise Lost, which recounts the story of "Man's First Disobedience" (Bk. I, l. 1) and his "loss of Eden" (Bk. I, l. 4). Paradise Lost, however, balances its account of the tragedy of the Fall with its description of the possibility of redemption by "one greater Man" (Bk. I, l. 4), and its conclusion balances the sorrow of the exile from Eden with the promise of happiness to come:

> Some natural tears they dropp'd, but wip'd
> them soon;
> The World was all before them, where to
> choose

> Thir place of rest, and Providence thir
> guide:
> They hand in hand with wand'ring steps
> and slow
> Through Eden took thir solitary way.
> (Bk. XII, ll. 645-49)

Guthlac B's bleak picture of exile balances Guthlac A's emphasis on joy, redemption, and the "eðel" (l. 67a) [homeland], which can refer either to an earthly homeland or to Paradise. Although Guthlac lives apart from other men, Guthlac A emphasizes that by so doing he has found his "eorð-lic eþel" (l. 261a) [homeland on earth]. Because he abandons the world for the better homeland of his hermitage, Guthlac is one of the saintly people who go to Heaven, the "eþellond / fæger 7 gefealic" (ll. 656b-57a) [fair and joyous native land]. Guthlac A's emphasis on the regained homeland is as incomplete as Guthlac B's emphasis on the miseries of the Fall, and only by reading the two together do we find the balance of regret for the Fall and expectation of the Redemption found in a work like Paradise Lost.

Finally, the two sections provide a balance of joy and sorrow, although the sorrowful side of life is emphasized because Guthlac B, elegiac in tone and mournful in subject, follows Guthlac A, which is filled with joy. Guthlac B ends with the lament of Guthlac's bereaved disciple and his statement that he is departing "hyge drusendne" (l. 1379b) [with a drooping mind]. Since medieval literature usually describes sorrow and lamentation as a necessary part of life, Guthlac B provides a corrective balance to Guthlac A, which is characterized by a uniformly joyous tone, and especially to its last word, "wynne" (l. 818b) [joy or pleasure]. Guthlac A ends with heavenly rejoicing and focuses our attention on the greatness of the saint's victory. In addition, it emphasizes the desirability of the eremitical life and the glory of the salvation which a hermit can confidently expect. This preternatural joy is, however, only part of what human beings experience, and it is balanced by the sombre picture presented by Guthlac B, which emphasizes the pain and sorrow of life and which reminds us that we are, indeed, all fallen with Adam and must drink "bryþen . . . / þætte Adame Eue gebyrmde / æt fruman worulde" (ll. 980b-82a) [the drink which Eve brewed for Adam at the beginning of the world]. The material in Guthlac B which describes the Fall thus provides a warning for us: salvation is possible for us as it was for Guthlac, but, because we are descendants of Adam, we must endure all the consequences of the Fall. Even though Guthlac B mentions Guthlac's ascension into Heaven, its emphasis is on human and worldly matters, and it ends by describing the disciple's grief. As a result, part of the effect of Guthlac is a warning that unless we lead a life like that Guthlac has led, we will fail to win a victory comparable to his.

As we have seen, Guthlac balances a joyous description of Guthlac's triumphant apotheosis against a sombre description of death and bereavement. The balance does not produce as dramatic an effect as does that in Beowulf, which contrasts such themes as youth and age, the beginnings and ends of dynasties, and fortitudino and sapientia. Instead, the two halves of Guthlac provide a completely static balance, and Guthlac B makes a more vivid impression on the reader only because it is the second. Guthlac has a high level of conscious literary sophistication; however, such sophistication does not necessarily mean it has great emotional appeal to a modern reader not particularly interested in the lives of the saints, especially in view of the fact that the pleasant themes of joy, hope, and salvation are in the first section but are obscured by the second section's description of death, exile, and sorrow. Guthlac is, nevertheless, an effective hagiographic narrative because it is didactic and provides pictures of a saint's life, the nature of sanctity, and both the good and evil sides of human life.

Section C
Guthlac: The Composite View

Both as a hagiographic narrative and as a poem written in the tradition inherited from oral epic, Guthlac may be considered part of the Old English poetic corpus, a different poem from either Guthlac A or B. Guthlac briefly describes the history of the world, and its emphasis, like that of Guthlac B which forms a part of it, is Orosian rather than Augustinian. However, it uses historical materials for a different purpose than does Guthlac B. The latter emphasizes the two major events of human history, the Fall and the Redemption, and shows that Guthlac re-enacts the cyclical pattern of each in his own life. The former intermingles events from all periods of human history and distorts linear time by placing its description of the Last Judgment before that of the Creation and Fall. All events of human history--past, present, and future--become part of Guthlac's life, and, by extension, of the life of every member of the poem's audience. Like the Libri Septem, Guthlac emphasizes that human life is a perennial cycle in which sorrow and death follow life and joy, and it adjures the members of its audience to abandon the "lænan dreamas" (l. 3a) [transitory joys] of this world and put their trust in God.

It is more difficult to assess the literary artistry of Guthlac than that of Guthlac A and B because, as far as a modern reader can tell, it was formed by the combination of the other two poems either at some date after their composition or, if the compiler was the author of Guthlac B who intended to compose a section to balance the already-extant Guthlac A, at the time of the composition of Guthlac B. I am inclined to suspect that the compiler was not the author of Guthlac B because the joyful theology of Guthlac A is so different from the grim Orosian theology of Guthlac B that I find it difficult to believe that the author of the latter would have had any interest in the former or would have wished his work to be combined with it. Since the matter is unresolvable at this time, the modern reader can only say that the text of Guthlac, as it appears in the manuscript, suggests that the two sections were chosen to complement each other and that therefore the artistry is that of the compiler rather than that of the author of an original work.

Guthlac presents a fuller picture of Guthlac's life and ministry than do either of the separate poems. It operates as a balance of opposing but related themes: saintly apotheosis and human grief, the other-worldly view of human history and the human view, and joy and sorrow. Because it places the sombre events of Guthlac B after the joyous events of Guthlac A, it reminds us that human life is sorrowful and that mankind's only hope lies in trusting God as Guthlac has done, and it eliminates the ineffable joy which makes the ending of Guthlac A resemble that of The Divine Comedy rather than the endings of extant Old English poems. As a result, Guthlac is in the mainstream of Old English poetry, which places its emphasis on the inexorable destruction of things valued by human beings. Guthlac resembles the Old English elegies by showing that, as The Seafarer points out, man's only hope lies in God:

>   Dol bið se þe him his dryhten ne ondrædeþ;
>   cymeð him se deað unþinged.
>   Eadig bið se þe eaþmod leofaþ;
>   cymeð him seo ar of heofonum,
>   meotod him þæt mod gestaþelað,
>   forþon he in his meahte gelyfeð.
>   (ll. 106a-8b)

[Foolish is he who does not fear his Lord; death comes to him unexpected. Blessed is he who lives humble; grace comes to him from Heaven, the Measurer makes his mind steadfast, because he believes in His might.]

Because Guthlac ends with a description not of the joys which the redeemed experience in Heaven but of the misery of Guthlac's disciple, it suggests that salvation is difficult to achieve and seems to echo Christ's words, "Multi enim sunt vocati, pauci vero electi" (Matthew 22:14) [For many are indeed called, but few are chosen]. The themes of Exile and the grim Cliff of Death in Guthlac A are balanced by the ominous theme of the Hero on the Beach in Guthlac B to produce a heightened sense of the gloomy fate of mankind in the post-lapsarian world. The compiler who juxtaposed themes seemingly designed to connote the inexorableness of fate and tragedy in human life and thus produced a new yet typical hagiographic poem showed a sensitivity to the uses of the traditional language and imagery of Old English poetry similar to that of the authors of Guthlac A and B who used the language and images to produce their idiosyncratic literary works.

Notes to Chapter Four

¹Modern critics disagree about how many poems Guthlac comprises. In Codex Exoniensis: A Collection of Anglo-Saxon Poetry (London: William Pickering, 1842), Benjamin Thorpe presents the Guthlac material as three separate poems: lines 1-29 "Of Souls After Death, etc., II," lines 30-92 "Poem Moral and Religious," and lines 93-1379 "The Legend of St. Guthlac" (pp. 102-84). Critics now agree that lines 819 through 1379 is one poem and that the material preceding line 819 comprises either one poem (lines 1 through 818) or two (lines 1 through 29 and 30 through 818). It would be possible to agree with Thorpe that the material between lines 30 and 92 is not part of Guthlac A and thus identify four separate poems, but most critics agree that there are two.

²Roberts, "A Metrical Examination of the Poems Guthlac A and Guthlac B," Proceedings of the Royal Irish Academy, 71 (1971), Sect. C, no. 4, p. 93.

³Roberts, "Metrical Examination," p. 119.

⁴Margaret E. Goldsmith, The Mode and Meaning of Beowulf (London: Athalone Press, 1970), p. 257.

⁵In The Guthlac Poems, pp. 12-19, Roberts discusses the practices of modern editors of the Exeter Book and points out that the 1857-58 edition by Christian W. M. Grein is the reason "for the consecutive numbering of the poems" (p. 17). Although she believes that Guthlac cannot be read as a composite, she numbers the poems consecutively.

⁶Calder, "Guthlac A and Guthlac B," p. 66.

⁷Robert Scholes and Robert Kellogg, The Nature of Narrative (London, Oxford, and New York: Oxford Univ. Press, 1975), pp. 21-22. All further references appear in the text.

[8] Oliver Goldsmith, "The Traveler," in <u>Collected Works of Oliver Goldsmith</u>, ed. Arthur Friedman, vol. 4 (Oxford: At the Clarendon Press, 1966), p. 236.

[9] Blake, ed., <u>The Phoenix</u>, p. 2.

[10] The editions of works discussed but not quoted in this section are <u>La Chanson de Guillaume</u>, ed. D. McMillan, 2 vols., Société des Anciens Textes Français, vol. 85 (Paris: Firmin Didot, 1949-50); <u>Raoul de Cambrai</u>, ed. P. Meyer and E. Lognon, Société des Anciens Textes Français, vol. 44 (Paris: Firmin Didot, 1882); <u>Aliscans</u>, ed. F. Guessard and A. de Montaiglon, <u>Les Anciens Poètes de la France</u>, vol. 10 (Paris: Viewig, 1870); <u>Chevalerie Vivien</u>, ed. R. Weeks (St. Louis: Univ. of Missouri, 1912); Guillaume de Lorris and Jean de Meung, <u>Le Roman de la Rose</u>, ed. Francisque Michel (Paris: Librairie de Firmin Didot, Frères, Fils, et Cie, 1864); <u>Grettis Saga Asmundarsonar</u>, ed. Guðni Jónsson, Islenzk Fornrit, vol. 7 (Reykjavík: Hið Íslenzka Fornritafélag, 1936); and <u>Vǫlsunga Saga</u>, ed. Magnus Olsen (København: S. L. Møllers Bogtrykkeri, 1906-8).

[11] In "Metrical Examination," Roberts examines the differences between the lines of <u>Guthlac</u> A and B in depth, discussing differences in anacrusis, contraction and syncopation, alliteration, and verse patterns.

[12] This theme is familiar to Anglo-Saxonists from the story of Cynewulf and Cyneheard in <u>The Anglo-Saxon Chronicle</u> for 755 A.D., John Earle and Charles Plummer, eds., <u>Two of the Saxon Chronicles Parallel</u>, rev. ed., vol. 1 (Oxford: At the Clarendon Press, 1965), pp. 47 and 49.

[13] Calder, "<u>Guthlac</u> <u>A</u> and <u>Guthlac</u> <u>B</u>," p. 66.

[14] Roberts, "A, B, and C," p. 44.

[15] See, for example, Joseph Bédier, <u>Les Légendes Épiques: Recherches sur la Formation des Chansons</u>

de Geste (Paris: Librairie Honoré Champion, 1914), vol. 1, pp. 82-97.

[16] In "Narrative Anomalies in La Chançun de Willame," Viator, 9 (1978), pp. 251-64, John D. Niles has suggested that the poem is coherent given the nature of oral poetry; he applies a Proppian analysis to the poem and concludes that it is not a composite but a work by a single poet.

[17] William C. Calin, The Old French Epic of Revolt: Raoul de Cambrai-Renaud de Montauban-Gormond et Isembart (Geneva: Librairie E. Droz, 1962), p. 13. All further references appear in the text. Another example of modern belief in "organic unity" is found in Robert's statement that Guthlac A and B "can well be read in sequence, but not as a single narrative with linear progression" (p. 49). As I argued in chapter one, Old English poems are static rather than linear; therefore, one cannot dismiss the possibility of reading Guthlac as a composite merely because it lacks "linear progression."

[18] See J. Rychner, La Chanson de Geste: Essai sur l'Art Epique des Jongleurs, Société de Publications Romanes et Françaises, vol. 53 (Geneva: Librairie E. Droz, 1955), pp. 46-47.

[19] Gerard J. Brault, "The French Chansons de Geste," Oinas, Heroic Epic and Saga, p. 193. All further references appear in the text.

[20] Delehaye, Légendes, pp. 14-15. His ideas on oral transmission are colored by his contempt for "la nature simpliste du génie populaire" (p. 17).

[21] James Whitby Earl, "Literary Problems in Early Medieval Hagiography" (Diss. Cornell Univ., 1971), p. 7. Many critics who believe that a typical hagiographic work exists seem to base that judgment on familiarity with only a few major hagiographic works, such as Sulpicius Severus' Vita Beati Martini, Gregory the Great's Dialogorum

Libri Quattuor, and Bede's Vita Sancti Cuthberti.
These works are so closely modelled on Athanasius'
Vita Sancti Antonii that they borrow not only ideas
and episodes but also entire passages therefrom.
As a result of the similarities, even scholars like
Jones tend to speak of "the fixed structure which
Evagrius and Sulpicius provided for . . . other
authors" (p. 65).

[22] Roberts, "An Inventory of Early Guthlac Materials," MS, 32 (1970), p. 205.

[23] Bertram Colgrave, "The Earliest Saints' Lives Written in England," Proceedings of the British Academy, 44 (1958), p. 55.

[24] Felix, Life of Saint Guthlac, pp. 16-17.

[25] Quoted by Colgrave in Felix, Life of Saint Guthlac, p. 17.

[26] Edgar J. Goodspeed, A History of Early Christian Literature, rev. Robert M. Grant (Chicago: The Univ. of Chicago Press, 1966), p. 64.

[27] Calder, "Guthlac A and Guthlac B," p. 66.

[28] Pontius Diaconus Carthaginensis, Vita et Passio Sancti Cæcilii Cypriani Episcopi Carthaginensis et Martyris, ed. J.-P. Migne, Patrologiae Cursus Completus, vol. 3 (Paris: Garnier Fratres, 1886), col. 1542. All further references appear in the text, and all translations are mine. I am not suggesting that the Vita Cypriani influenced the compiler of Guthlac, but merely that it is typical of Patristic works which describe the life and passion of a martyr. Ogilvy's Books Known to the English indicates that there is no evidence that Pontius' Vita itself was known in Anglo-Saxon England.

[29] Gerould has suggested that the poems we now call Guthlac A and B might appropriately be entitled "Guthlac the Hermit . . . [and] Guthlac's Death" ["The Old English Poems on St. Guthlac," p. 77],

although since he views the poems as separate he does not notice that the composite forms a Vita et Passio.

[30] Renoir, "Roland's Lament," pp. 572-83.

[31] F. Whitehead, ed., La Chanson de Roland, ll. 2393-96 (Oxford: Basil Blackwell, 1968), p. 70.

Conclusion
The Artistry of the Guthlac Poems

     As the foregoing discussion has argued, from
a pragmatic point of view, the Exeter Book Guthlac
may be said to comprise three poems, Guthlac A,
Guthlac B, and Guthlac. All three are hagiographic works which describe incidents from the life of
St. Guthlac, although none is fully biographical.
Despite the omnipresence of formulaic elements in
the Guthlac poems, many scholars have discussed
only their literary and theological backgrounds.
Furthermore, no one--not even a critic like Goldsmith who recognizes that the placement of Guthlac
A and B in the manuscript suggests that they were
intended to be read as a unit--has discussed Guthlac, the composite poem. The technique that this
study has suggested has been to examine the poems
in the light of both traditions that influenced
them, so that we are able to read them in a way
more sympathetic to them than has been possible
hitherto. Furthermore, when reading the materials
with both the hagiographic and the oral-formulaic
traditions in mind, we are able to realize that
the two original poems were at some time combined
into a single work of literary merit.

     Guthlac A has often been criticized because
it is didactic, but an understanding of the nature
and purpose of hagiography shows that all hagiographic works, even those which are generally
considered literary masterpieces, are didactic.
It is not enough, however, to view Guthlac A as
merely a versified theological treatise because it
is also a poem. Guthlac A develops by repetition
and balance and uses formulas and themes to express its religious subject. In addition, it has
a mythic level which adds resonance to both the
religious themes and the heroic language in which
the former are depicted. From the point of view
of literary artistry, Guthlac A is an effective
poem.

Guthlac B has been incorrectly assessed because critics have failed to note that its philosophical background is Orosian rather than Augustinian and have decided that it is not an effective poem although they praise its use of the formulaic devices of composition. Guthlac B shows a remarkably able use of both the Germanic and the Patristic literary traditions insofar as it uses the theme of the Hero on the Beach in a way which permits readers to observe the fulfillment of a pattern which they anticipate because it occurs in both hagiography and heroic poetry. Guthlac B can only be appreciated by one who reads it as a work which is both hagiographic and heroic.

Furthermore, if we read the Guthlac material in the light of both traditions which lie behind it, we realize that, although Guthlac A and B were undoubtedly composed separately, it is possible to read Guthlac as the scribe of our only manuscript probably intended it to be read: as a single poem about Guthlac. Guthlac is a narrative which develops by repetition and balance and which uses many formulaic devices of composition. It is a reasonable hagiographic narrative that provides more details about Guthlac's life than do either Guthlac A or B, and the two may have been combined to provide such full details.

On both pragmatic and literary grounds, the Guthlac materials can be read as three Old English poems: Guthlac A, Guthlac B, and Guthlac. In order to understand fully the Old English poems based on Latin models, we must consider whether they use the formulaic elements of Old English heroic poetry effectively to express the religious ideas derived from Latin works. All three Guthlac poems are effective, for each blends elements from two disparate traditions into new and exciting forms. I should like to suggest that, if students of Old English poetry were to use this composite technique, they would be able to develop new readings of the other hagiographic poems as well: Andreas, Juliana, Judith, and Elene.

Bibliography

Ælfric. *Homilies of Ælfric: A Supplementary Collection.* 2 vols. Ed. John C. Pope. EETS, Old Series vols. 259 and 260. London, New York, and Toronto: The Early English Text Society, 1968.

———. *The Homilies of the Anglo-Saxon Church.* 2 vols. Ed. and trans. Benjamin Thorpe. London: The Ælfric Society, 1844 and 1845.

Albertson, Clinton J., S. J. *Anglo-Saxon Saints and Heroes.* New York: Fordham Univ. Press, 1967.

Anderson, George K. *The Literature of the Anglo-Saxons.* Princeton, New Jersey: Princeton Univ. Press, 1949.

Bédier, Joseph. *Les Légendes Épiques: Recherches sur la Formation des Chansons de Geste.* 4 vols. Paris: Librairie Honoré Champion, 1914.

Benedict, Abbot of Monte Cassino. *Commentary on the Holy Rule of St. Benedict.* Ed. and trans. Dom Justin McCann. 2nd. ed. London: Burns and Oates, 1959.

Benson, Larry D. "The Literary Character of Anglo-Saxon Formulaic Poetry." *PMLA*, 81 (1966), pp. 334-41.

Bessinger, J. B., Jr. *A Concordance to the Anglo-Saxon Poetic Records.* Ithaca and London: Cornell Univ. Press, 1978.

Biblia Sacra. Vulgatae Editionis. Rome: Editiones Paulinae, 1957.

Biebuyck, Daniel P. "The African Heroic Epic."
 *Heroic Epic and Saga: An Introduction to the
 World's Great Folk Epics.* Ed. Felix J. Oinas.
 Bloomington and London: Indiana Univ. Press,
 1978.

Black, Robert P. "Some Notes and Queries on the
 Uses of Irony." In *Geardagum II: Essays on
 Old and Middle English Language and Literature.* Ed. Loren C. Gruber and Dean Loganbill.
 Denver: The Society for New Language Study,
 1978, pp. 54-60.

Blake, N. F., ed. *The Phoenix.* Manchester: Manchester Univ. Press, 1964.

Blomfield, Joan. "The Style and Structure of
 Beowulf." *Review of English Studies,* 14
 (1938). Rpt. in *The Beowulf Poet: A Collection of Critical Essays.* Ed. Donald K. Fry.
 Englewood Cliffs, New Jersey: Prentice-Hall,
 Inc., 1968, pp. 57-65.

Bonjour, Adrien. "*Beowulf* and the Beasts of Battle." *PMLA,* 72 (1957), pp. 563-73.

Bosworth, Joseph, ed. *An Anglo-Saxon Dictionary.*
 Enlarged by T. Northcote Toller with revised
 and enlarged addenda by Alister Campbell.
 Oxford: The Univ. Press, 1973.

Bötticher, Gotthold, ed. and trans. *Hildebrandlied und Waltharilied nebst den "Zaubersoruchen" und "Muspilli."* Dentmäler der Älteren Deutschen Literatur. Ed. Gotthold
 Bötticher and Karl Kinzel. Vol. 1. Halle:
 Verlag der Buchhandlung des Waisenhauses,
 1905.

Brault, Gerard J. "The French Chansons de Geste."
 *Heroic Epic and Saga: An Introduction to the
 World's Great Folk Epics.* Ed. Felix J.
 Oinas. Bloomington and London: Indiana
 Univ. Press, 1978, pp. 193-215.

Bugge, John. "The Virgin Phoenix." MS, 38 (1976), pp. 332-50.

Calder, Daniel G. "Guthlac A and Guthlac B: Some Discriminations." Anglo-Saxon Poetry: Essays in Appreciation, for John C. McGalliard. Ed. Lewis E. Nicholson and Dolores Warwick Frese. Notre Dame, Indiana: Notre Dame Univ. Press, 1975, pp. 65-80.

_____. "Theme and Strategy in Guthlac B." PLL, 8 (1972), pp. 227-42.

Calin, William C. The Old French Epic of Revolt: Raoul de Cambrai-Renaud de Montauban-Gormond et Isembart. Geneva: Librairie E. Droz, 1962.

Chambers, R. W., Max Förster, and Robin Flower, eds. The Exeter Book of Old English Poetry. London: Percy, Lund, Humphries, and Co., 1933.

Chaucer, Geoffrey. The Works of Geoffrey Chaucer. Ed. F. N. Robinson. 2nd. ed. Boston: Houghton Mifflin Co., 1961.

Cherniss, Michael D. Ingeld and Christ: Heroic Concepts and Values in Old English Christian Poetry. The Hague: Mouton, 1972.

Colgrave, Bertram. "The Earliest Saints' Lives Written in England." Proceedings of the British Academy, 44 (1958).

_____. Ed. and trans. Two Lives of St. Cuthbert: A Life by an Anonymous Monk of Lindisfarne and Bede's Prose Life. New York: Greenwood Press, 1969.

Cornell, Cynthia Edelstein. "Sources of the Old English Guthlac Poems." Diss. Univ. of Missouri-Columbia, 1976.

Crépin, André. "Bede and the Vernacular." _Famulus Christi: Essays in Commemoration of the Thirteenth Centenary of the Birth of the Venerable Bede_. Ed. Gerald Bonner. London: SPCK, 1976, pp. 170-92.

Crowne, David K. "The Hero on the Beach: An Example of Composition by Theme in Anglo-Saxon Poetry." _NM_, 61 (1960), pp. 362-72.

Dante Alighieri. _The Divine Comedy: Paradiso_. Vol. 1. Ed. and trans. Charles S. Singleton. Bollingen Series. Vol. 80. Princeton, New Jersey: Princeton Univ. Press, 1975.

Delehaye, Hippolyte. _Les Légendes Hagiographiques_. 3rd. ed. Subsidia Hagiographica. Vol. 18. Bruxelles: Société des Bollandistes, 1927.

──────. _Les Origines du Culte des Martyrs_. 2nd. ed. Subsidia Hagiographica. Vol. 20. Bruxelles: Société des Bollandistes, 1933.

──────. _Les Passions des Martyrs et les Genres Littéraires_. 2nd. ed. Subsidia Hagiographica. Vol. 13B. Bruxelles: Société des Bollandistes, 1966.

Du Lorris, Guillaume and Jean de Meung. _Le Roman de la Rose_. Ed. Francisque Michel. Paris: Librairie de Firmin Didot Frères, Fils, et Cie, 1864.

Earl, James Whitby. "Literary Problems in Early Medieval Hagiography." Diss. Cornell Univ., 1971.

Earle, John and Charles Plummer, eds. _Two of the Saxon Chronicles Parallel_. 2 vols. Rev. ed. Oxford: At the Clarendon Press, 1965.

Eliade, Mircea. _The Myth of the Eternal Return, or, Cosmos and History_. Trans. Willard R. Trask. Bollingen Series 46. Princeton, New Jersey: Princeton Univ. Press, 1974.

Farrell, R. T. "Some Remarks on the Exeter Book 'Azarias'." MÆ, 41 (1972), pp. 1-8.

Felix. <u>Life</u> <u>of</u> <u>St</u>. <u>Guthlac</u>. Ed. and trans. Bertram Colgrave. Cambridge: The Univ. Press, 1956.

Foley, John Miles. "Formula and Theme in Old English Poetry." <u>Oral</u> <u>Literature</u> <u>and</u> <u>the</u> <u>Formula</u>. Ed. Benjamin A. Stolz and Richard S. Shannon, III. Ann Arbor: Center for the Coördination of Ancient and Modern Studies, 1976, pp. 207-32.

French, Walter Hoyt and Charles Brockway Hale. <u>The</u> <u>Middle</u> <u>English</u> <u>Metrical</u> <u>Romances</u>. 2 vols. New York: Russell and Russell, Inc., 1964.

Fry, Donald K. "Caedmon as a Formulaic Poet." <u>Forum</u> <u>for</u> <u>Modern</u> <u>Language</u> <u>Studies</u>, 10 (1974), pp. 227-47.

_____. "The Cliff of Death in Old English Poetry." Unpublished.

_____. "The Heroine on the Beach in <u>Judith</u>." <u>NM</u>, 68 (1967), pp. 168-83.

Gerould, Gordon Hall. "The Old English Poems on St. Guthlac and Their Latin Source." <u>MLN</u>, 32 (1917), pp. 77-89.

Goldsmith, Margaret E. <u>The</u> <u>Mode</u> <u>and</u> <u>Meaning</u> <u>of</u> <u>Beowulf</u>. London: Athalone Press, 1970.

Goldsmith, Oliver. <u>Collected</u> <u>Works</u> <u>of</u> <u>Oliver</u> <u>Goldsmith</u>. Ed. Arthur Friedman. 5 vols. Oxford: At the Clarendon Press, 1966.

Goodspeed, Edgar J. <u>A</u> <u>History</u> <u>of</u> <u>Early</u> <u>Christian</u> <u>Literature</u>. Rev. Robert M. Grant. Chicago: The Univ. of Chicago Press, 1966.

Goodwin, Charles Wycliffe, ed. and trans. <u>The</u> <u>Anglo-Saxon</u> <u>Version</u> <u>of</u> <u>the</u> <u>Life</u> <u>of</u> <u>St</u>. <u>Guth-</u>

lac, Hermit of Croyland. London: John
Russell Smith, 1848.

Gordon, R. K., trans. Anglo-Saxon Poetry. London:
J. M. Dent and Sons, Ltd., 1970.

Greenfield, Stanley B. A Critical History of Old
English Literature. 2nd. Printing. New
York: New York Univ. Press, 1968.

_____. "The Formulaic Expression of the Theme
of 'Exile' in Anglo-Saxon Poetry." Speculum,
30 (1955), pp. 200-6.

Grein, Christian W. M. Bibliothek der Angelsächischen Poesie. Vol. 3. Leipzig: George H.
Wigand, 1897.

Guessard, F. and A. de Montaiglon. Aliscans. Les
Anciens Poètes de la France. Vol. 10.
Paris: Viewig, 1870.

Hanning, Robert W. "Beowulf as Heroic History."
Medievalia et Humanistica, Series 2, 5
(1974), pp. 77-102.

_____. The Vision of History in Early
Britain: From Gildas to Geoffrey of Monmouth. New York: Columbia Univ. Press,
1966.

Herzfeld, George, ed. and trans. An Old English
Martyrology. EETS, Old Series vol. 116.
London: The Early English Text Society,
1900. Rpt. Millwood, New York: Kraus Reprint Co., 1975.

Hill, Thomas D. "The Typology of the Week and the
Numerical Structure of the Old English Guthlac B." MS, 37 (1975), pp. 531-36.

Hoare, F. R., trans. The Western Fathers. The
Makers of Christendom, ed. Christopher Dawson. London: Sheed and Ward, 1954.

Holthausen, Ferdinand. *Altenglisches Etymologisches Wörterbuch*. 2nd. ed. Heidelberg: Carl Winter, 1963.

Huffines, Marion Lois. "OE *aglaece*: Magic and Moral Decline of Monsters and Men." *Semasia*, 1 (1974), pp. 71-81.

Irving, Edward B., Jr. "Image and Meaning in the Elegies." *Old English Poetry: Fifteen Essays*. Ed. Robert P. Creed. Providence, Rhode Island: Brown Univ. Press, 1967, pp. 153-66.

Jones, Charles W. *Saints' Lives and Chronicles in Early England*. Ithaca, New York: Cornell Univ. Press, 1947.

Jónssǫn, Guðni, ed. *Grettis Saga Ásmundarsonar*. Íslenzk Fornrit. Vol. 7. Reykjavík: Hið Íslenzka Fornritafélag, 1936.

Joseph of Arimathea. *De Transitu Beatae Mariae Virginis*. *Apocalypses Apocryphae*. Ed. Konstantine von Tischendorf. Hildeshein: Georg Olms Verlagsbuchhandlung, 1966, pp. 113-23.

Kennedy, Charles William. *The Earliest English Poetry*. New York and London: Oxford Univ. Press, 1943.

Klaeber, Friedrich, ed. *Beowulf and the Fight at Finnsburg*. 3rd. ed. with 1st. and 2nd. supplements. Boston: D. C. Heath and Co., 1950.

Kobos, Chester. "The Structure and Background of *Guthlac A*." Diss. Fordham Univ., 1972.

Krapp, George Philip and Elliott Van Kirk Dobbie, eds. *The Anglo-Saxon Poetic Records*. 6 vols. New York: Columbia Univ. Press, 1931, 1932, 1936, 1953, 1932, and 1942. Rpt. 1969.

Kurtz, Benjamin P. "From St. Anthony to St. Guthlac: A Study in Biography." *Univ. of California Publications in Modern Philology*, 12 (1926), pp. 103-46.

Langen, Toby Christopher. "A Commentary on the Two Old English Poems on St Guðlac." Diss. Univ. of Washington, 1973.

Lefebvre, Gaspar, O. S. B., ed. *Daily Missal*. St. Paul, Minnesota: E. M. Lohmann Co., 1925.

Lipp, Frances Randall. "Guthlac A: An Interpretation." *MS*, 33 (1971), pp. 46-62.

Lord, Albert B. *The Singer of Tales*. Harvard Studies in Comparative Literature, 24 (1960). Rpt. New York: Atheneum, 1974.

Magoun, Francis P., Jr. "Oral-Formulaic Character of Anglo-Saxon Narrative Poetry." *Speculum*, 28 (1953), pp. 446-67.

Malone, Kemp. *The Middle Ages: The Old English Period*. A Literary History of England. Vol. 1. Ed. Albert C. Baugh. New York: Appleton-Century-Crofts, 1967.

Mason, James David. "Monsters with Human Voices: The Anthropomorphic Adversary of the Hero in Old English and Old Norse Literature." Diss. Univ. of Tennessee, 1976.

McMillan, D., ed. *La Chanson de Guillaume*. 2 vols. Société des Anciens Textes Français. Vol. 85. Paris: Firmin Didot, 1949-50.

Meyer, P. and E. Lognon, eds. *Raoul de Cambrai*. Société des Anciens Textes Français. Vol. 44. Paris: Firmin Didot, 1882.

Milton, John. *Complete Poems and Major Prose*. Ed. Merritt Y. Hughes. New York: The Odyssey Press, 1957.

Morris, R., ed. and trans. The Blickling Homilies of the Tenth Century. EETS, Old Series vols. 58, 63, and 73, in one volume. London: The Early English Text Society, 1880.

Morris, Richard, ed. Cursor Mundi: Four Versions. EETS, Old Series vols. 57, 59, 62, 66, 68, and 99. 6 vols. Oxford: The Early English Text Society, 1874, 1875, 1876, 1877, 1878, and 1892. Rpt. 1961.

Nagler, Michael N. Spontaneity and Tradition: A Study in the Oral Art of Homer. Berkeley, Los Angeles, and London: Univ. of California Press, 1974.

Niles, John D. "Narrative Anomalies in La Chançun de Willame." Viator, 9 (1978), pp. 251-64.

Ogilvy, J. D. A. Books Known to the English, 597-1066. Cambridge, Massachusetts: Mediaeval Academy of America, 1967.

Olsen, Alexandra Hennessey. "'De Historiis Sanctorum': A Generic Study of Hagiography." Genre, 13 (1980), 407-29.

_____. "Guthlac on the Beach." Neophilologus, 64 (1980), pp. 290-96.

Olsen, Magnus, ed. Vǫlsunga Saga. København: S. L. Møllers Bogtrykkeri, 1906-8.

Ong, Walter, S. J. "Oral Residue in Tudor Prose Style." Rhetoric, Romance, and Technology: Studies in the Interaction of Expression and Culture. Ithaca and London: Cornell Univ. Press, 1971, pp. 23-47.

Orm. The Ormulum with the Notes and Glossary of Dr. R. M. White. 2 vols. Ed. Robert Holt. Oxford: At the Clarendon Press, 1878.

Opland, Jeff. Anglo-Saxon Oral Poetry: A Study

of the Traditions. New Haven and London: Yale Univ. Press, 1980.

Orosius, Paulus. Historiarum Adversum Paganos Libri Septem, Accedit Eiusdem Liber Apologeticus. Ed. Carolus Zangemeister. Corpus Scriptorum Ecclesiasticorum Latinorum. Vol. 5. Vindobonae: C. Geroldi Filium Bibliopolam Academiae, 1882.

Palumbo, Edward M. The Literary Use of Formulas in Guthlac II and Their Relation to Felix's Vita Sancti Guthlaci. The Hague and Paris: Mouton, 1977.

Parry, Milman. "Studies in the Epic Technique of Oral Verse-Making I: Homer and Homeric Style." Harvard Studies in Classical Philology, 41 (1930), pp. 73-147.

_____. "Studies in the Epic Technique of Oral Verse-Making II: The Homeric Language as the Language of Oral Poetry." Harvard Studies in Classical Philology, 43 (1932), pp. 1-50.

Pontius, Diaconus Carthaginensis. Vita et Passio Sancti Cæcilii Cypriani Episcopi Carthaginensis et Martyris. Patrologiae Cursus Completus, vol. 3. Ed. J.-P. Migne. Paris: Garnier Fratres, 1886, cols. 1541-58.

Post, Thomas R. "The Benedictine Influence on Guthlac A." Unpublished.

Propp, Vladimir. Morphology of the Folktale. Trans. Laurence Scott. Rev. Louis A. Wagner. Austin and London: Univ. of Texas Press, 1975.

Reichardt, Paul F. "Guthlac A and the Landscape of Spiritual Perfection." Neophilologus, 58 (1974), pp. 331-38.

Renoir, Alain. "Beowulf: A Contextual Introduction to Its Contents and Techniques." *Heroic Epic and Saga: An Introduction to the World's Great Folk Epics*. Ed. Felix J. Oinas. Bloomington and London: Indiana Univ. Press, 1978, pp. 99-119.

_____. "The Kassel Manuscript and the Conclusion of the Hildebrandslied." *Manuscripta*, 23 (1979), pp. 104-8.

_____. "Oral-Formulaic Theme Survival: A Possible Instance in the 'Nibelungenlied'." *NM*, 65 (1964), pp. 70-75.

_____. "Roland's Lament: Its Meaning and Function in the Chanson de Roland." *Speculum*, 35 (1960), pp. 572-83.

Roberts, Jane. "Guðlac A, B, and C?" *ME*, 42 (1973), pp. 43-46.

_____. *The Guthlac Poems of the Exeter Book*. Oxford: Clarendon Press, 1979.

_____. "An Inventory of Early Guthlac Materials." *MS*, 32 (1970), pp. 192-233.

_____. "A Metrical Examination of the Poems Guthlac A and Guthlac B." *Proceedings of the Royal Irish Academy*, 71 (1971), Sect. C, No. 4, pp. 91-137.

Robinson, Fred C. "Some Uses of Name-Meanings in Old English Poetry." *NM*, 69 (1968), pp. 161-71.

Rosier, James L. "Death and Transfiguration: Guthlac B." *Philological Essays in Old and Middle English Literature and Language in Honor of Herbert Dean Merritt*. Ed. James L. Rosier. Paris: Mouton, 1970, pp. 82-92.

Rychner, J. *La Chanson de Geste: Essai sur l'Art Epique des Jongleurs*. Société de Publications

Romanes et Françaises. Vol. 53. Geneva: Librairie E. Droz, 1955.

Scholes, Robert and Robert Kellogg. The Nature of Narrative. London, Oxford, and New York: Oxford Univ. Press, 1975.

Shook, Lawrence K. "The Burial Mound in Guthlac A." MP, 58 (1960), pp. 1-10.

_____. "The Prologue of the Old-English 'Guthlac A'." MS, 23 (1961), pp. 294-304.

Spenser, Edmund. Poetical Works. Ed. J. C. Smith and E. De Selincourt. London: Oxford Univ. Press, 1966.

Sulpicius Severus. De Vita Beati Martini, Liber Unus. Patrologiae Cursus Completus. Vol. 20. Ed. J.-P. Migne. Paris: Venit Apud Editorem, 1845, cols. 159-76.

Thormann, Janet. "Variations on the Theme of the 'Hero on the Beach' in 'The Phoenix'." NM, 71 (1970), pp. 187-90.

Thorpe, Benjamin, ed. Ancient Laws and Institutes of England. 2 vols. England: The Commissioners on the Public Records of the Kingdom, 1840.

_____. Codex Exoniensis: A Collection of Anglo-Saxon Poetry. London: William Pickering, 1842.

_____. Tha Halgan Godspel on Englisc: The Anglo-Saxon Version of the Holy Gospels. 2nd. ed. New York: George P. Putnam, 1848.

Thundyil, Zacharias P., C. M. I. Covenant in Anglo-Saxon Thought. Madras, Bombay, Calcutta, and Delhi: The Macmillan Co. of India, Ltd., 1972.

Tolkien, J. R. R. "Beowulf: The Monsters and the

Critics." *Proceedings of the British Academy*, 22 (1936), pp. 245-95. Rpt. in *An Anthology of Beowulf Criticism*. Ed. Lewis E. Nicholson. Notre Dame: Univ. of Notre Dame Press, 1963, pp. 51-104.

Watts, Ann Chalmers. *The Lyre and the Harp, A Comparative Reconsideration of Oral Tradition in Homer and Old English Epic Poetry*. New Haven: Yale Univ. Press, 1969.

Weeks, R., ed. *Chevalerie Vivien*. St. Louis: Univ. of Missouri, 1912.

Wentersdorf, Karl P. "Guthlac A: The Battle for the Beorg." *Neophilologus*, 62 (1978), pp. 135-42.

Whitehead, F., ed. *La Chanson de Roland*. Oxford: Basil Blackwell, 1968.

Whitman, F. H. "The Meaning of 'Formulaic' in Old English Verse Composition." *NM*, 76 (1975), pp. 529-37.

Wolpers, Theodor. *Die Englische Heiligenlegende des Mittelalters*. Tübingen: Max Niemeyer, 1964.

Woolf, Rosemary. "Saints' Lives." *Continuations and Beginnings: Studies in Old English Literature*. Ed. Eric Gerald Stanley. London: Thomas Nelson and Sons, Ltd., 1966, pp. 37-66.

Wrenn, Charles L., ed. *Beowulf with the Finnesburg Fragment*. 2nd. ed. London: George C. Harrap Co., Ltd., 1958.

_____. *Beowulf with the Finnesburg Fragment*. Rev. Whitney F. Bolton. New York: St. Martin's Press, 1973.

Wülcker, Richard P. "Über den Dichter Cynewulf." *Anglia*, 1 (1878), pp. 483-507.

Wulfstan. *Sermo Lupi Ad Anglos*. Ed. Dorothy
    Whitelock. London: Methuen and Co., Ltd.,
    1939.

Index

Ælfric   12, 16, 84-85, 87, 106, 120
Ælfwald   65
Æthewold, Bishop   20
Albertson, Clinton   3-4, 54
Aldhelm   120
Anderson, George K.   25, 69, 71
Anglo-Latin Works   Bede, Historia Ecclesiastica 16-17; Vita Sancti Cuthberti 16, 66, 120, 121, 138; Eddius Stephanus, Vita Sancti Wilfrithi Episcopi 121; Felix, Vita Sancti Guthlaci 2, 17, 33, 47-48, 65-66, 70-73, 79, 82-83, 93, 95, 97-98, 100-1, 103, 119, 120, 121
Assumption of Mary   38

Beccel   82-83, 91, 102
Bédier, Joseph   136-37
Benson, Larry D.   1, 94
Bessinger, J. B., Jr.   11-12
Biblia Vulgata   Colossians 2:20 126; Job 43; John 14:27 87; Liber Regum Quartus 2:11 128; Luke 4:34-35 21, 22:42 20; Mark 2:5 84-85; Matthew 22:14 134; Romans 5:17-19 125; Old English Version of Matthew 106
Biebuyck, Daniel P.   12
Black, Robert P.   60, 106
Blake, N. F.   136
Blomfield, Joan   26
Bollandists, The   2
Bolton, Whitney F.   62
Bonjour, Adrien   55, 99
Bosworth, Joseph   61
Brault, Gerard J.   120, 123, 137
Bugge, John   43-44

Calder, Daniel G.   1, 22, 24, 30, 54-55, 59, 69, 72, 78, 86, 88, 105, 112, 121, 136
Calin, William C.   117, 118, 120
Chaucer, Geoffrey   The Canterbury Tales 72
Cherniss, Michael D.   3, 25, 35, 43, 79, 95

Colgrave, Bertram   65, 103, 120
Comitatus   45
Cornell, Cynthia Edelstein   20, 65, 95, 101
Crépin, André   57
Crowne, David K.   95, 99, 103
Cursor Mundi   61
Cynewulf   12, 107, 112

Dante Alighieri   The Divine Comedy   56, 133
Delehaye, Hippolyte   9-10, 118, 137

Earl, James Whitby   119
Eliade, Mircea   47-48, 49
Elijah   128

Farrell, R. T.   90
Foley, John Miles   94-95
Fry, Donald K.   1, 6, 13, 94, 95-96, 97-98

Gerould, Gordon Hall   64, 138-39
Goldsmith, Margaret E.   111, 141
Goldsmith, Oliver   113
Goodspeed, Edgar J.   121
Gordon, R. K.   22, 58
Greenfield, Stanley B.   50, 69, 71-72, 94, 101
Grein, Christian W. M.   58, 135

Hanning, Robert W.   2, 65
Herzfeld, George   17
Hildebrandlied, The   99, 100, 108
Hill, Thomas D.   11
Holthausen, Ferdinand   59
Homer   The Iliad   108;   The Odyssey   49-52

Irving, Edward B.   1

John Cassian   54
Johnson, Samuel   113
Jones, Charles W.   2, 7, 16, 17, 64, 119, 120, 138

Kennedy, Charles William   101
Kobos, Chester   64
Krapp, George Philip and Elliott Van Kirk Dobbie
    11, 22, 59

Kurtz, Benjamin P.   105

Langen, Toby Christopher   38, 54, 71, 88, 90-91, 102
Lipp, Frances Randall   15, 18
Lord, Albert B.   1, 7, 9, 12-13, 94, 105

Magoun, Francis P., Jr.   1, 4, 9, 59-60
Malone, Kemp   64
Mason, James David   40-42, 117
Milton, John   Paradise Lost   8, 21, 129-30
Myth of the Eternal Return, The   49-52, 54

Nagler, Michael N.   49
Niles, John D.   137

Ogilvy, J. D. A.   62, 138
Old English Manuscripts   The Exeter Book   1, 22, 111-12, 113, 114, 142; The Vercelli Book   18
Old English Poetry   Aldhelm   17; Andreas   8, 99, 121, 142; Azarias   90; The Battle of Brunanburh   12; Beowulf   19, 26, 29, 31-32, 33-34, 35-36, 37, 40, 41, 46, 55, 70, 71, 124, 131; Christ II   7-8, 12, 100, 111; Christ III   22, 111; Christ and Satan   13, 27, 36, 124; Daniel   7, 30; The Dream of the Rood   18-19; Elene   8, 12, 92-93, 99, 121, 142; Exodus   99; The Fates of the Apostles   12; The Fight at Finnsburh   96; Genesis A   12; Genesis B   21, 36, 41, 75-76; Judith   6, 8, 36-37, 38, 40, 55, 96, 99, 102, 142; Juliana   8, 121, 142; The Lord's Prayer II   12; Pharaoh   90; The Phoenix   17, 43-44, 51, 63, 74-75, 94, 99; The Seafarer   133; A Summons to Prayer   17; The Wanderer   91, 101
Old English Prose   Ælfric, Sermo de Die Iudicii   12; The Anglo-Saxon Chronicle   136; The Anglo-Saxon Version of the Holy Gospels   106; The Old English Life of Saint Guthlac   65, 98; The Old English Martyrology   17; The Pœnitentiale Ecgberti Archepiscopi Eboracensis   30, 61; The Thirteenth Blickling Homily   38, 63
Old French Poetry   Aliscans   116; La Chanson de Guillaume   115-16, 121; La Chanson de Roland

46, 128-29; Chevalerie Vivien 116; Raoul
de Cambrai 115-16; Le Roman de la Rose 112,
117
Old Norse Works   Fáfnismál 117; Grettis Saga
116-17; Reginsmál 117; Sæmundar Edda 112;
Vǫluspá 42; Vǫlsunga Saga 117
Ong, Walter J.   5
Opland, Jeff   12
Oral-Formulaic Themes   The Beasts of Battle 99;
The Cliff of Death 8, 13, 55, 100, 134;
Exile 39, 43, 55, 63, 134; The Hero on the
Beach 95-101, 102-4, 142
Ordericus Vitalis   119
Orm   The Ormulum   61

Palumbo, Edward M.   10-11
Parry, Milman   1, 9
Patristic Works   Athanasius, Vita Sancti Antonii
70, 73, 119, 120, 138; Augustine, De Civitate
Dei 72, 92; Benedict, Regula Monachorum 20,
53-54; Boethius, De Consolatione Philosophiae
124; Gregory the Great, Dialogorum Libri
Quattuor 120, 137-38; Jerome, Vita Pauli
120; Lactantius, Carmen de Ave Phoenice 99;
Orosius, Historiarum Adversum Paganos Libri
Septem 72-93, 101-2, 132; Passiones 70,
122; Pontius, Vita et Passio Sancti Cæcilii
Cypriani 122-23, 138; Sulpicius Severus,
Vita Sancti Martini 35, 137; Visio Sancti
Pauli 54; Vita Cyriaci 121
Post, Thomas R.   20, 54
Propp, Vladimir   50

Reichardt, Paul F.   34, 54
Renoir, Alain   5, 26, 60, 96, 108, 128
Robert of Sicily   39
Roberts, Jane   11, 58, 64, 90, 107, 111, 135, 136,
137
Robinson, Fred C.   18
Rosier, James L.   70-72, 79
Rychner, J.   117

Saints   Augustine 81, 91; Bartholomew 18, 29,
37, 43, 50, 127, 128; Benedict 20, 101;

Cuthbert 6, 119, 120; Cyprian 122-23; Gregory the Great 101; Martin 24; Oswald 120; Pega 89, 100; Swithin 119
Scholes, Robert and Robert Kellogg 112, 123
Shook, Lawrence K. 15, 25, 34, 54
Spenser, Edmund The Faerie Queene 24
Sulpicius Severus 23-24

Thormann, Janet 99
Thorpe, Benjamin K. 24, 135
Thundyil, Zacharias P. 20, 54, 58
Tolkien, J. R. R. 26, 46

Virgil 120

Watts, Anne Chalmers 10
Wentersdorf, Karl P. 34
Whitman, F. H. 9
William of Malmesbury 119
Wolpers, Theodor 57, 69, 71
Woolf, Rosemary 4, 15, 17-18, 25, 70, 72, 91
Wrenn, Charles L. 62
Wülcker, Richard P. 107
Wulfstan 16, 30-31